simply
beautiful

ribbon Craft

heidi boyd

NORTH LIGHT BOOKS
CINCINNATI, OHIO
www.artistsnetwork.com

09 08 07 06 05   5 4 3 2 1

Library of Congress Cataloging-in-Publication Data
Simply beautiful ribboncraft: 50 quick and easy projects / Heidi Boyd.
    p. cm.
Includes index.
ISBN 1-58180-592-6 (alk. paper)
  1. Ribbon work. I. Title.

TT850.5.B67 2005
746".0476--dc22
               2004065428

Editors: Jolie Lamping Roth and David Oeters
Designer: Marissa Bowers
Layout Artist: Jessica Schultz
Production Coordinator: Robin Richie
Photographers: Al Parrish, Tim Grondin, Hal Barkan and Christine Polomsky
Photo Stylists: Jan Nickum and Nora Martini

F+W PUBLICATIONS, INC.

metric conversion chart

TO CONVERT	TO	MULTIPLY BY
Inches	Centimeters	2.54
Centimeters	Inches	0.4
Feet	Centimeters	30.5
Centimeters	Feet	0.03
Yards	Meters	0.9
Meters	Yards	1.1
Sq. Inches	Sq. Centimeters	6.45
Sq. Centimeters	Sq. Inches	0.16
Sq. Feet	Sq. Meters	0.09
Sq. Meters	Sq. Feet	10.8
Sq. Yards	Sq. Meters	0.8
Sq. Meters	Sq. Yards	1.2
Pounds	Kilograms	0.45
Kilograms	Pounds	2.2
Ounces	Grams	28.4
Grams	Ounces	0.04

ABOUT THE
author

Artist **HEIDI BOYD** creates innovative craft projects for both children and adults, emphasizing the elements of surprise and accessibility. In addition to **SIMPLY BEAUTIFUL RIBBONCRAFT**, Heidi has authored **SIMPLY BEAUTIFUL BEADING**, **SIMPLY BEAUTIFUL GREETING CARDS**, **WIZARD CRAFTS**, **PET CRAFTS** and **FAIRY CRAFTS**, all published by North Light Books. She's contributed proprietary projects to **BETTER HOMES AND GARDENS** magazines and craft books.

With a degree in fine arts, Heidi has taught workshops and art classes in schools and art centers for more than a decade. She lives in Maine with her husband, two sons and dog.

DEDICATED TO...

For fellow crafters, who just can't sit still and are compelled to keep your hands busy creating. Your enthusiasm is infectious! I love to hear from you and meet you at signings and demonstrations.

Working countless hours in the studio is a solitary occupation. I'm especially grateful for the encouragement and support of Karina Illingworth, Mellissa Orth, Claudia Brzoza, Deb Merrill, Sylvia Wyler, Candee Kaknes, Poppy Arford, Hannah Beattie and Patti Michaud.

acknowledgments • Thanks to Jolie Lamping Roth for getting this book rolling and to David Oeters who picked it up and got it to print. Christine Polomsky who graciously helped me through yet another marathon photo shoot. Marissa Bowers, who truly made this book Simply Beautiful. Sally Finnegan for her crucial role in getting my books onto store shelves. I'm always grateful for the talents of photo stylists and proofreaders who quietly play an integral role in making a quality publication.

contents

introduction

if you've ever taken the time to save a ribbon from a package, lingered over a ribbon display in a fabric store, or even riffled through an old drawer of cast off ribbons, then you've experienced their attraction first hand. Like fabrics, they come in an endless variety of colors, but what makes ribbons uniquely appealing is their lush, silky texture. They're simply irresistible to the touch. Some elaborate varieties feature an exquisite mixture of metallic and translucent fibers with wire edges making them ideal for crafting. Others have intricate patterns of swirling hearts and flowers woven with tiny silken threads. I find their beautiful detail a source of visual fascination.

Making crafts with ribbons has never been easier. My objective in designing projects for this book was to take advantage of many ribbon varieties and find simple techniques to transform them into useful crafts. In just an evening crafters can be rewarded with a beautiful finished project. Eliminating the need to sew, both double-sided craft tape and fusible web quickly became the indispensable tools to my ribbon crafting success. They effortlessly attach ribbon to glass, metal, fabric and paper without the mess and drying time associated with glues.

Whether you enjoy jewelry making, card making, scrapbooking or embellishing fabric, ribbons can be easily incorporated into your creations. Extremely versatile, the endless array of ribbon varieties, colors and sizes makes it easy to find the perfect ribbon for any

application. I've shared ways to personalize your home décor by fusing ribbons to fabric to create elegant pillow covers, sachets and table linens. I've experimented with laying ribbon flat, tying it in bows and ruffling it before attaching it to paper to make handcrafted cards. Paired with beautiful glass, stone and silver beads, ribbons make stunning feminine chokers, necklaces, barrettes and headbands.

This book is intended for everyone. Absolutely no prior knowledge in bow tying or sewing is required. You'll find easy-to-follow instructions for each step. Before you know it you'll have impressed family and friends with a stunning array of ribbon crafts, decorations and gifts. Like untying a ribbon wrapped present, I hope this book unfolds to offer you hours of inspiration and creative enjoyment.

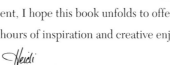

ribbon

Beautiful ribbon is everywhere and with each season the selection grows as different fibers, patterns and colors are incorporated into new designs. Ribbon can easily be found in both craft and fabric stores. You can even find ribbon in many scrapbook and beading stores.

purchasing

If you need a small amount of expensive ribbon, I suggest purchasing it by the foot. Otherwise, it's usually more economical to buy a whole spool (or package) of ribbon. Check out the selection of specialty holiday ribbon on sale after the season has passed. This is a great time to stock up and expand your collection.

Look for reds and pinks in the spring, pastels in early summer, red, white and blue at the end of the summer, black and harvest colors in early winter and silver and gold metallics after New Year's. When you see a design or color you like, don't hesitate to purchase it. There's no guarantee that the design will remain on the market. Be on the lookout for unique vintage ribbons salvaged from milliners' and dressmakers' studios. Most importantly, amass colors and varieties of ribbons that inspire you to create.

storage

Nothing is as frustrating as reaching into a pile of ribbon searching for a certain color ribbon, only to find it completely tangled and knotted with other ribbon. I suggest using a rubber band or small piece of tape to prevent opened ribbon spools from unwinding. Line ribbon spools into a plastic storage bin, or thread them onto a homemade hanging rack made with dowel rods. Both storage solutions ensure that colors are easy to locate and the ribbon is accessible.

types of ribbon

Here's a sampling of different ribbons to help familiarize you with the basic features of each variety. This should help you locate the appropriate ribbon for each project in the book.

You can always select a different ribbon color, but in most cases the type and size of ribbon is crucial to the ease of re-creating the craft. For instance, wire-edged ribbon is ideal for creating ribbon flowers. The wires hold the shaped petal in place, but the same wire makes the ribbon a bad choice for machine stitching.

Many ribbons are difficult to classify as they share aspects of two or even three different varieties. For instance, a holiday ribbon may be velvet and have metallic gold edges that are wired, or an organdy ribbon may also have satin strips. When dealing with hybrid ribbons just make sure the ribbon you choose has the integral characteristic neccessary to make the project work. For example, you might prefer to wrap metallic ribbon around the glass votive candleholder. This substitution will work as long as the ribbon is still sheer enough to let candlelight pass through.

| **FEATHERED EDGE** | The fibers along the top and bottom edges of the ribbons have been pulled out into a pattern of loops. The decorative edge makes the ribbon appear wider than it actually is. | **BROCADE** | A wide, heavyweight ribbon that is distinguished by repeated decorative motifs. Usually woven in rich jewel tones and commonly used in home decorating projects. | **SATIN** | Silky smooth, this common ribbon features the widest selection of widths and color shades. | **DOUBLE-SIDED RIBBON** | Unlike satin ribbon, double-sided ribbon is equally shiny on both sides. Sometimes this ribbon features two separate solid colors, with one on each side.

| **ORGANDY** | The sheerest of ribbons, it allows light to pass through with the subtlest tints of color. | **WIRE-EDGED** | Thin wires can be invisibly woven into the edges of almost any kind of ribbon. The wire allows the positioned ribbons to hold their shape. This ribbon isn't intended to be laundered, and is most frequently used in flower arranging. | **METALLIC** | Shiny threads create a metallic ribbon that reflects light. Sometimes metallic fibers are only incorporated though the center or sides of the ribbon. | **JACQUARD** | Jacquard ribbon has a woven pattern that repeatedly runs through the length of the ribbon. The woven threads only make a pattern on one side of the ribbon. The multiple threads tend to increase the thickness of the ribbon. | **GINGHAM AND PLAID RIBBONS** | The checked pattern is woven into the ribbon and is clearly visible on both the front and back. Gingham ribbons are traditionally red or black paired with white. They're lightweight and feel like satin. | **GROSGRAIN** | Grosgrain is a sturdy woven ribbon that has a flat matte finish. It's distinguished by tight vertical ridges that run across the ribbon.

RIBBONS

printed ribbon

beaded fringe

| **BEADED FRINGE** | ¼" (6mm) or ⅛" (3mm) wide satin ribbon tops most beaded fringe. Repeated strands of seed beads with sequins or crystals hang from the bottom edge of the ribbon. It's sold by the yard at fabric stores or in packages at craft supply stores. | **VELVET** | Velvet ribbon features soft fibers on the topside and flat woven ribbon on the underside. It's most commonly found in deep blue and black colors and is sold almost exclusively in fabric stores. | **POLKA DOT AND PRINTED RIBBON** | The top side of these ribbons is stamped with a pattern. The under side is usually plain.

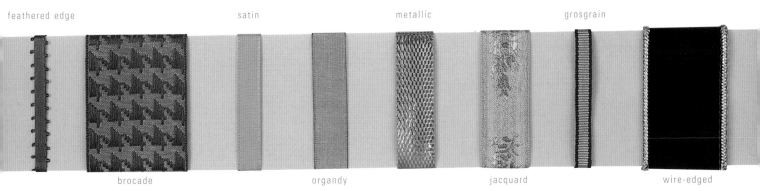

feathered edge   satin   metallic   grosgrain

brocade   organdy   jacquard   wire-edged

tools

When shopping for supplies, I'm always stumbling upon appealing new tools that make crafting even easier. New products appear on the market all the time. What you'll find below is a sampling of tools and some tips on how to get the most out of your tools. Remember, if you can't find the exact tool mentioned below, there are plenty of products that will work just as well, if not better.

adhesives

aleene's 2 in 1

| **ALEENE'S 2 IN 1** | Perfect for gluing lightweight paper projects as it allows you to reposition items before permanently adhering them in place. | **MEMORY GLUE** | This craft glue is strong enough to glue scrapbook embellishments to most surfaces. The narrow applicator tip makes it easy to position the glue exactly where you need it and controls the glue flow to prevent it from pooling. It dries flat and will not buckle the paper surface. | **ALEENE'S PLATINUM BOND TEXTILE GLUE** | This heavy-duty adhesive is perfect for permanently adhering embellishments to ribbon. | **BEACON'S CRAFTFOAM GLUE** | It's difficult to secure foam pieces with traditional adhesives. I strongly suggest using glue that is formulated especially for this purpose. | **BEACON'S HOLD THE FOAM GLUE** | This product is formulated to work with porous Styrofoam surfaces. Using products like this will give you peace of mind that your projects will last longer. | **MOD PODGE** | This classic découpage medium is simply brushed over ribbon and paper to adhere it to the desired surface. | **HOT GLUE** | Ideal for an instant bond, hot glue easily holds lightweight items together. | **DOUBLE-SIDED CRAFT TAPE** | Craft tape simplifies adhering ribbons to almost every surface. Liquid glue can seep through the porous ribbon fabric, but craft tape tightly bonds the ribbon in place. Available in a variety of widths starting at ⅛" (3mm). Look for this heavy-duty adhesive where craft and scrapbook supplies are sold. Don't substitute standard double-sided office tape. | **FUSIBLE WEB TAPE** | Position fusible tape between ribbon and fabric and then activate the adhesive by ironing the layers together. You can find this product in fabric stores. | **CLEAR NAIL POLISH** | While not an adhesive, it can be applied to cut ribbon edges to prevent the threads from fraying. I find the built-in brush and thick polish easy to control. If you prefer, you can substitute Fraycheck liquid seam sealant.

memory glue

fusible web tape

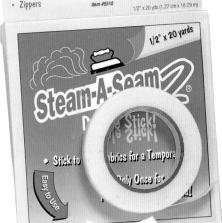

decoupage medium

aleene's platinum bond textile glue

tools

You'll need very few tools to get ready for ribboncrafting. Many of these are used in scrapbooking and jewelry crafting as well. Don't hesitate to invest in these relatively inexpensive and versatile items. | **SCISSORS** | Sharp scissors are crucial to the success and ease of crafting with both fabric and ribbon. Dull scissors won't make a clean cut and will fray the ribbon ends. I use a variety of Fiskars scissors. Long shears for cutting fabric, and smaller tips for trimming thread ends and making tight cuts. My personal favorite is Softouch scissors, which have a central spring and require little pressure to make a cut. | **PAPER TRIMMER** | This handy tool makes cutting paper to exact measurements a breeze. It's perfect for cutting paper to cover boxes and make cards. | **IRON** | Breathe second life into wrinkled ribbons. Press them flat so they look like new. Use low heat and a press cloth to prevent scorching the ribbon. | **AWL** | This is a useful tool for pre-punching stitching holes or creating openings for rivets. | **SMALL CRAFT HAMMER** | This lightweight hammer is perfect for flattening eyelets and firmly snapping rivets together. | **EYELET SETTER** | Match the size of the eyelet setter to the selected eyelet. Exert force on the setter with a craft hammer. | **WIRE CUTTER** | Don't nick your scissors blades by using them to cut wire. Wire cutters are both safer and easier to use. They are especially handy for cutting through heavy wire-cored floral stems. | **NEEDLE-NOSE PLIERS** | Jewelry projects require shaping and manipulating wire and findings with needle-nose pliers. | **HOLE PUNCHES** | Fiskars makes good quality paper punches. I frequently use the ⅛" (3mm) and ¼" (6mm) sized hole punches when paper crafting. They make ideal sized holes for threading thin ribbons.

tip > As with any sewing project, it is important to press the fabric. Ribbon has crease lines when it's sold packaged around cardboard. It takes just seconds to iron and flatten it. Ironing ribbon also renews recycled or tangled ribbons. Use the silk setting on your iron and work on a protected surface. The trick is to quickly pull the ribbon out from under the iron to avoid scorching it.

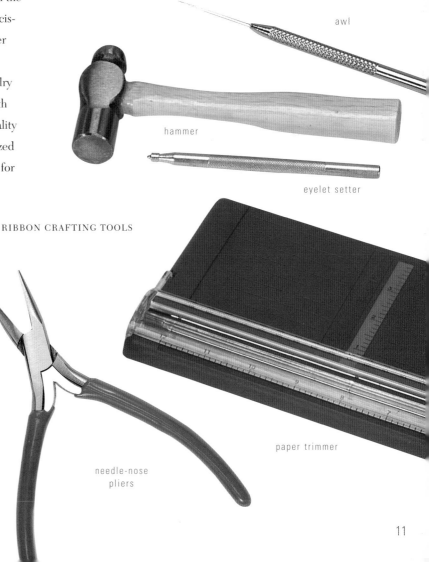

RIBBON CRAFTING TOOLS

scissors

hole punch

awl

hammer

eyelet setter

needle-nose pliers

paper trimmer

tip > Be sure to finish the ribbon ends after you've completed a project, otherwise they'll fray. Apply a thin line of clear nail polish along the cut ribbon edge. The polish doesn't disappear when it dries, so it's important to apply as little as possible while still trapping the cut fibers. Wipe the brush against the bottle rim to remove excess polish.

techniques

Crafting with ribbon is much easier than you might think. These quick and easy techniques will help you get the most from your ribbon and start crafting simply beautiful projects.

tying a bow

This classic bow tying technique makes the most attractive ribbon bows. So if you're someone who cheats and ties two loops together, revisit these steps to make beautiful ribbon bows.

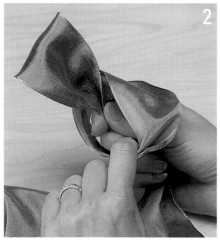

one • Form a ribbon loop, making it the size that you will need for the project. Hold the ends in one hand. This loop will become the left side of the bow.

two • Bring the left ribbon end up, over and around the bottom of the loop to form the center of the bow.

three • Pull this same ribbon out through the right side of the newly formed bow center to make the right side of the bow. Do not pull the ribbon all the way through. You should have formed another loop.

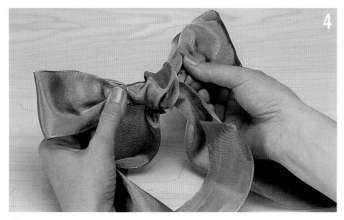

four • Pull evenly on both bow loops to tighten the center of the bow. If necessary, pull on each loop separately to even the size of the loops.

trimming ribbon ends

You have many options when trimming the ends of your ribbons. Below are three different options. Don't hesitate to switch to another of these options for any of the projects in this book. Before trimming any tied bow, line up the ends or measure them to cut the ribbons at equal lengths.

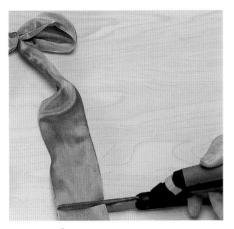

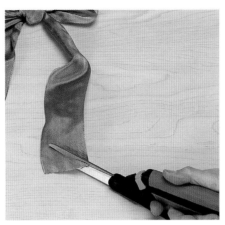

straight · Cut straight across the ribbon ends to make even horizontal lines.

diagonal · Cut the ribbon ends diagonally, making one side the mirror image of the other. The longer ribbon edges should line up with the sides of the bow and the shorter edges will fall below the center of the bow. The angle of the cut will affect the finished length of the ribbon.

notch · Fold the ribbon in half and then cut through both layers at a diagonal angle towards the fold. The notch is revealed when the ribbon is unfolded. The appearance of this technique can vary depending on how deep or shallow you cut the notch. Make an identical notch on the other ribbon end.

ruffling

This technique looks more complicated than it is. You don't need to be an experienced ribbon crafter to ruffle ribbon, and the results are beautiful.

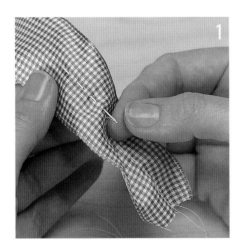

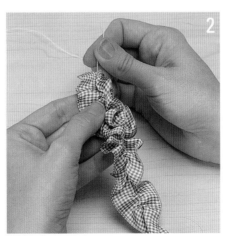

one · Thread a sewing needle with a generous amount of thread and leave the end unknotted. Make a simple straight stitch down the center of the ribbon length.

two · While holding the needle in one hand, slide the ribbon toward the thread end. If you need more ruffles at the base, hold the thread ends and slide the ribbon up. You can easily loosen or tighten the ruffles to expand or shrink the length of the ribbon. Once the ruffle is manipulated to the desired length, cut off the needle and knot the thread ends.

three · Ribbon rosettes are made using the same ruffling technique with one variation; the stitches are sewn up one edge of the ribbon. If you use a two-colored ribbon, then the finished flower will be the color of the unstitched side.

home accents

i t's the individual decorating touches that truly make your home unique. Use the ribbon crafts in this section to accent your personal decorating style. The variety of ribbon colors, patterns and styles makes it easy to coordinate projects with your existing décor.

The throw pillows and rickrack table set are a cinch to make and perfect for someone new to the craft of sewing. Both use purchased table linens so the edges are already professionally sewn. Not prepared to try sewing at all? Fool your friends with the following projects that cleverly mimic the appearance of sewn ribbon by using double-sided craft tape. Display treasured photos in a wooden frame that is gilded in metallic ribbon. Flower topped boxes are a beautiful way to stash odds and ends while creating a decorative focal point on end tables and bureaus. Set a romantic mood with flickering light from an organdy ribbon votive holder.

Looped ornate ribbon tassels add luxury to a room as they hang from armoires or curtains. Beautiful centerpiece flowers are quickly assembled with organdy ribbon and wire. Weave ribbons over the back of a clear glass plate to make an original decorative dish. An ornament of ribbon and crystal beads captures the light as it streams in your windows.

Turn the pages of this section and you're sure to find something simply beautiful to make your home décor reflect your creativity.

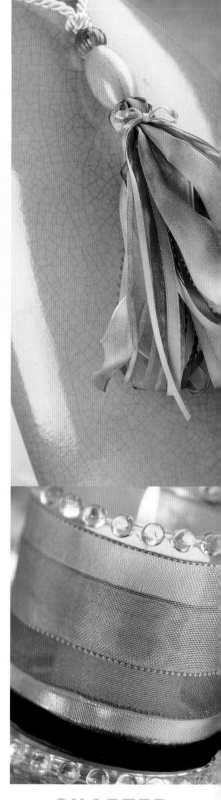

CHAPTER

1

gilded frame

photo frame

1" (3cm) wide brocade ribbon

¼" (6mm) gold wire-edged ribbon

¼" (6mm) blue satin ribbon

double-sided craft tape:
1" (3cm) and ½" (13mm) widths

Aleene's Memory Glue

NOTE: Tape width should match
the total ribbon width.

tip > This project is the perfect way to recycle chipped or scratched wood frames. If the scratches are on the inside edge of the frame, line the first ribbon against the inside edge. If the chips are on the outside corners, position the ribbon against the outside edge. The unblemished parts of the wood will remain visible, and damaged areas will be decoratively concealed.

Make an ordinary wood frame extraordinary with strips of ornate brocade, satin and metallic ribbons. The diagonal folding technique at the corners gives the ribbon a sewn appearance, but it's simply adhered with double-sided craft tape. This project can be easily adapted for different color schemes and frame sizes by matching the width of the double-sided craft tape to the width of the selected ribbons.

one · Apply a strip of 1" (3cm) wide double-sided craft tape to the outer edge of the frame, then apply a strip of ½" (13mm) wide double-sided craft tape against the inside edge of each 1" (3cm) tape strip. You should have a total of 1½" (4cm) of tape around the four sides of the frame, so the total tape width equals the total width of the ribbons you are using. Peel the backing off one of the 1" (3cm) wide tape pieces to expose the adhesive.

two · Place the 1" (3cm) wide brocade ribbon over the exposed adhesive. At the corners, fold the ribbon ends under and at an angle, then trim away excess ribbon. Peel the backing off an adjoining 1" (3cm) tape strip, and place another length of brocade into the adhesive. Fold both ends under at an angle. Make sure the new diagonal fold connects with the last folded ribbon corner. Repeat the process to attach brocade ribbon to the remaining two sides of the frame and complete three more corner connections.

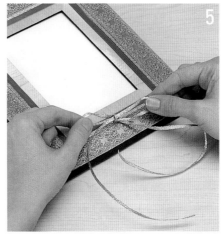

four · Place a length of the wire-edged ribbon between the brocade and the satin ribbons along the top of the frame. Do not fold the ribbon at the corners but make a diagonal cut. Place two more lengths of wire-edged ribbon down either side of the frame, diagonally cutting the corners so that they connect with the first ribbon.

five · Join two lengths of gold ribbon to the bottom of the frame, one at each corner. Bring the ribbons together, tie them into a small bow and trim the ends. If necessary, add a little glue under the cut ribbon corners to help them lie flat.

three · Peel the backing from one strip of the ½" (13mm) tape. Place the ¼" (6mm) blue ribbon along the outside edge of the ½" (13mm) tape strip, leaving a ¼" (6mm) space between the blue ribbon and the brocade ribbon placed in step 2. Fold both corners under at an angle. Repeat the process to attach the three remaining sides of the satin ribbon around the frame, connecting the diagonal folds at each corner.

tassels

MATERIALS

18" (46cm) silk cord

6' to 8' (1.5m to 2m) lengths of assorted varieties of ribbons: in widths from ⅛" (3mm) to 1½" (4cm)

large wooden bead

large glass bead

16" (41cm) of 26-gauge wire

Aleene's Textile Glue

12" (30cm) wooden ruler

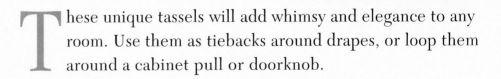

These unique tassels will add whimsy and elegance to any room. Use them as tiebacks around drapes, or loop them around a cabinet pull or doorknob.

ANOTHER SIMPLY BEAUTIFUL IDEA

This project brings new life to old ribbons. Combine remnants from old ribbon spools with new spools. The resulting mixture of ribbon varieties will create an interesting finished tassel.

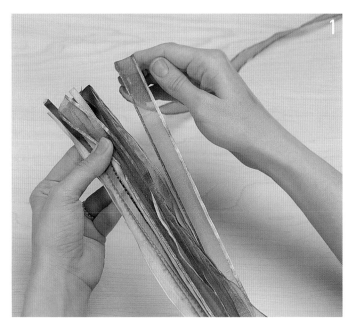

one · Wrap each ribbon variety three to four times around a ruler. Pinch the layers of wrapped ribbon against the ruler with one hand while adding new lengths of ribbon with the other hand.

two · Carefully slide the ribbons off the ruler leaving the looped shape intact. Wrap the center of the wire around the middle of the ribbons. Tightly twist the wires together above the ribbons. It's important that the wire prevent any loose ribbon ends from sliding out. Thread both wire ends through a wooden bead and a glass bead.

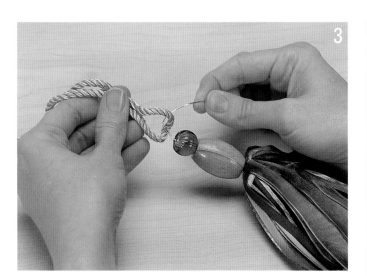

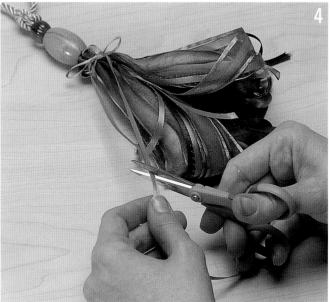

three · Wrap the wire around the center of the silk cord, and trim away the excess wire. Bring the cord ends together and tie them in an overhand knot. Slide the knot down the cord until it rests over the glass bead and conceals the wire connection, then pull the knot tight.

four · Tightly wrap a thin ribbon scrap around all the ribbon loops, ½" (13mm) below the wooden bead. Tie the ribbon into a bow and trim the ends so they're the same length as the looped ribbon. Bring the silk cord ends together and tie them in an overhand knot. To help prevent the cord ends from unraveling, squeeze a small amount of glue into the cut ends. With your fingertips, carefully twist the individual fibers into the glue.

votive candleholder

MATERIALS

glass votive candleholder [3" (8cm) in diameter and 3" (8cm) high]

10" (25cm) of 1⅜" (3cm) wide gold organdy ribbon

10" (25cm) of 1⅜" (3cm) wide red organdy ribbon

10" (25cm) of ¼" (6mm) wide gold metallic ribbon

10" (25cm) of ¼" (6mm) wide black velvet ribbon

½" (13mm) and ¼" (6mm) wide double-sided craft tape (heat resistant)

craft glue

clear nail polish

NOTE: Look for straight-sided glassware so the wrapped ribbons lie flat.

ANOTHER SIMPLY BEAUTIFUL IDEA

Transform clear glassware into stunning votive candle-holders. Layers of sheer ribbons filter candlelight to make a romantic focal point. Scent the room by lighting subtly fragrant candles. The glass will safely contain any melted wax.

To make a complete set of ribbon lights, select various sized glassware. Make use of any sheer ribbon scraps you may already own. Don't skip velvet ribbon, it adds contrast and drama to the otherwise sheer holder. Experiment with positioning the ribbons in different combinations before taping them to the glass.

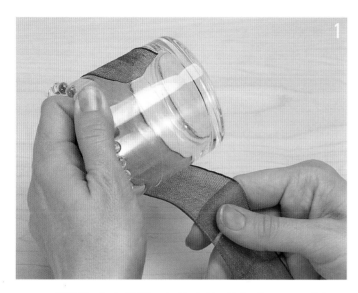

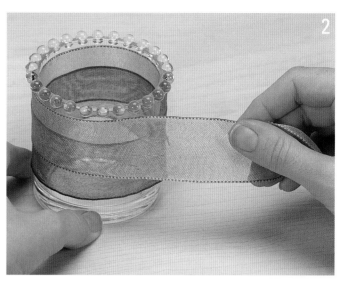

one · Apply ½" (13mm) wide double-sided craft tape around the center of the glass. Peel off the protective backing and wrap red organdy ribbon over the exposed adhesive. Carefully trim the ribbon end so it overlaps by ⅛" (3mm), then apply nail polish to the cut edge.

two · Apply a second band of ½" (13mm) wide double-sided craft tape under the lip of the glass. Peel off the protective backing and wrap the gold organdy ribbon over the exposed adhesive. The bottom edge of the gold ribbon should overlap the top edge of the red ribbon. Trim the ribbon end so it overlaps by ⅛" (3mm) and apply nail polish to the cut edge. If necessary, use a small piece of double-sided craft tape to secure the ribbon end flush against the wrapped ribbon.

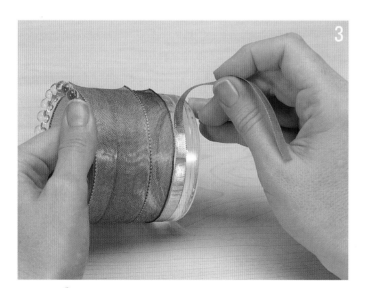

three · Apply a band of ¼" (6mm) wide double-sided craft tape below the red organdy ribbon on the glass. Peel off the backing and wrap the gold metallic ribbon over the exposed adhesive.

four · Apply a final band of ¼" (6mm) wide double-sided craft tape around the base of the votive, directly below the gold metallic ribbon. Peel off the backing and wrap the velvet ribbon over the exposed adhesive. Glue the end of the ribbon flush against the wrapped velvet.

flowers on top

MATERIALS

2½" (6cm) square by 1½" (4cm) tall
white papier mâché box

four 8" (20cm) pieces of ⅝" (6mm) wide
light purple ribbon

10" (25cm) of ⅜" (10mm) wide
grosgrain ribbon

2⅛" (5cm) square decorative paper

nine silk flowers (african violets)

¼" (6mm) wide double-sided craft tape

clear nail polish

glue gun

ANOTHER SIMPLY BEAUTIFUL IDEA

If you need a larger gift box simply select wider ribbon, and larger silk flowers, such as bachelor buttons, that will cover the additional surface.

Put your wrapping paper aside! Ribbon and silk flowers will quickly transform a plain cardboard box into a stunning gift box. These flower-topped boxes are the perfect way to present wedding favors. The flowers will spread blooming color over the reception tables.

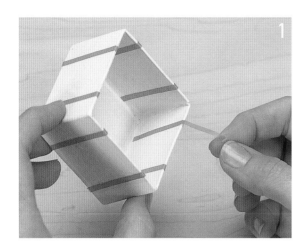

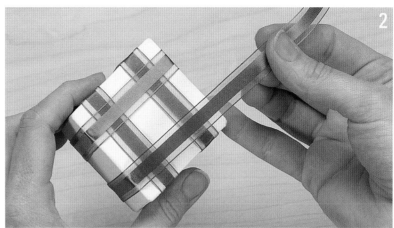

one · Apply eight strips of double-sided craft tape to the sides of the box. Position the end of each strip inside the box, bring the length of the tape over the top edge, then press the end of the tape down against the outside of the box. Place two tape strips on each side of the box. Don't place tape on the base of the box. Press all the positioned tape firmly in place, then peel off the backing.

two · Begin placing the four ⅝" (16mm) wide ribbon lengths over the exposed tape. Position the end of the first ribbon length inside the box, follow the tape over the side of the box, then stretch the ribbon across the base of the box. Lay the remaining ribbon against the tape on the other side of the box; end inside the box. Repeat the process, covering two taped sides and the underside of the box with the three remaining ribbon lengths.

three · Place the decorative paper square inside the box to cover the ends of the ribbon.

four · Cut the silk flower heads off the stems and hot glue three rows of three flowers onto the box lid.

five · Apply double-sided craft tape around the rim of the lid, then peel the backing off the tape. Lay the ⅜" (10mm) wide grosgrain ribbon over the exposed tape. Trim the end of the ribbon and apply clear nail polish to the cut end to prevent fraying.

berry sachets

MATERIALS

12½" (32cm) length and
10" (25cm) length of 3" (8cm) wide
multicolored wire-edged ribbon

floral fruit berries

fragrant sachet mix

cotton batting

glue gun

ANOTHER SIMPLY BEAUTIFUL IDEA

Coordinate the ribbon color with both the floral berries and fragrance pellets. For example, fill a purple ribbon sachet with blackberry fragrance and top it with floral blackberries. Make gift sachets for friends and family that are customized to match their favorite scents and colors.

Luscious and ripe for the picking, these scented sachets aren't seasonal. They'll keep their color and fragrance year-round. Using 3" (8cm) wide wire-edged ribbon is essential to the quick and simple no-sew assembly of this project.

one · Place a small handful of batting in the center of the 10" (25cm) length of ribbon.

two · Pour some fragrant sachet pellets into the center of the batting and place a second small handful of batting over the fragrance.

three · Bring the ribbon ends up over the top of the batting and hot glue one ribbon end over the other.

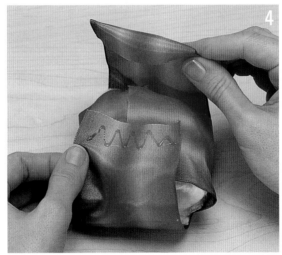

four · Place the bundle, glue side up, onto the center of the 12½" (32cm) length of ribbon. Bring the new ribbon ends up to cover the exposed batting on the sides of the bundle. Fold one of the cut ribbon ends under and then hot glue it over the other ribbon end.

five · Turn the sachet right side up, so the glued ribbon is on the bottom. Thread the wire end of the berries under the center of the top ribbon. Wrap the wire around the ribbon to gather the fabric and anchor the berries in place. Shape the wire ends by spiraling them around a pencil. If necessary, hot glue the sides of the ribbon together at the corners to prevent the batting from falling out.

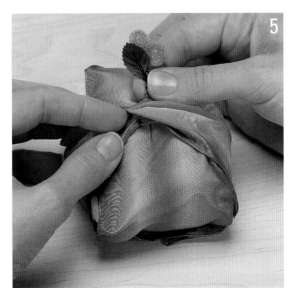

pillow

MATERIALS

three 20" (51cm) square cloth
napkins (two black, one tan)

18" (46cm) square pillow

six 19" (48cm) strips of
1½" (4cm) wide satin ribbon

sewing machine and thread

straight pins

clear nail polish

ANOTHER SIMPLY BEAUTIFUL IDEA

There's no end to the array of colored and patterned cloth napkins available in stores. Select patterns and coordinating ribbon to make pillows that complement your living room couch or your bedroom linens.

These clever pillows are a cinch to make. Gather three cloth napkins and sew them together with three straight seams. All the cloth edges are already finished. Simply slide a pillow form into the sleeve and tie the top and bottom flaps closed with ribbons. Untie the ribbons and slide out the pillow for easy washing.

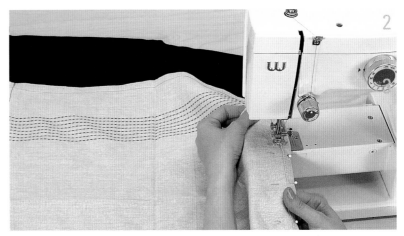

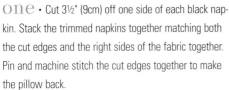

one · Cut 3½" (9cm) off one side of each black napkin. Stack the trimmed napkins together matching both the cut edges and the right sides of the fabric together. Pin and machine stitch the cut edges together to make the pillow back.

two · Unfold the stitched pillow back so it's right side up. The tan napkin becomes the pillow front; lay it right side down over the center of the pillow back. Pin the top and bottom of the pillow front and back together. Machine stitch a seam down the top and bottom of the pillow, removing the pins as you stitch. Turn the pillowcase right side out.

three · Machine stitch three ribbon lengths to each side of the black pillow back. Position the ribbons 4" (10cm) apart and 4" (10cm) from the top and bottom of the edges.

four · Slide the 18" (46cm) pillow into the open sides of the finished pillow cover.

five · Fold the flaps over the sides of the pillow and tie the ribbons into bows. Trim excess length off the ribbon ends and apply clear nail polish to the cut edges to prevent fraying.

hat box

MATERIALS

7" (18cm) x 2" (5cm) tall
papier mâché hat box

36" (91cm) of 1" (3cm) wide
satin green ribbon

1" (3cm) wide feather-edged
jacquard ribbon

floral patterned scrapbook paper
cut to cover box lid

red simulated wood patterned scrapbook
paper cut to cover box sides (if necessary, you can join two pieces of paper)

paper rose with floral wire stem

snap-on paper crafting rivets
(Scrapbook Rivets by Scrapbook Interiors)

Aleene's 2 in 1 glue

½" (13mm) double-sided craft tape

awl

small crafting hammer

ANOTHER SIMPLY BEAUTIFUL IDEA

This project can easily be adjusted to cover different sized boxes. Simply use the desired box as the pattern. Cut one paper variety to cover the box sides and another to cover the box top. Increase or decrease the width of the feather-edged jacquard ribbon to cover the rim of the box lid. Stick to white and ivory paper and ribbons for a wedding box, and pastel colors for a baby box.

This chic box is the perfect adornment for a bedroom dresser, where it serves as a beautiful catchall for odds and ends. A unique gift wrapping solution, this beautiful box stands apart from gift bags and traditionally wrapped packages.

one • Remove the box lid. Starting with the box base, glue red scrapbook paper around the sides. If necessary, trim any excess paper from around the top or bottom edge. Next, cover the box lid with the floral paper and trim any excess paper.

two • For positioning purposes place the lid on the box. Use an awl to punch a hole on either side of the box base midway between the lid rim and the bottom of the box. Trim away the broken cardboard around the holes. Thread a pair of snap rivets through each side of the holes. Hammer the snaps together so they're firmly anchored in place. Enlarge the hole if you're having trouble threading the snaps. If they don't snap together, remove more cardboard and try again.

four • Apply double-sided craft tape around the rim of the box lid. Peel off the protective backing to expose the adhesive. Wrap the 1" (3cm) wide jacquard ribbon around the rim and press it firmly into the adhesive.

five • Replace the box lid and bring both ribbon ends up over the sides of the box. Tie the ribbon ends into a bow over the center of the lid. Thread the flower stem through the middle of the finished bow. Don't tie the ribbon in a knot, as you'll need to open the box easily.

three • Thread one end of the 1" (3cm) wide satin ribbon through both holes in the box. Pull the ribbon end out through the second hole until both ribbon ends are equal in length, and the center of the ribbon rests inside the middle of the box. Trim the ends on the diagonal and apply clear nail polish to the cut edges to prevent fraying.

rickrack table set

MATERIALS

15" (38cm) in diameter red and
black round quilted place mat

19" (48cm) square
black fringed cloth napkin

17" (43cm) square red cloth napkin

1½" (4cm) in diameter
black lacquered napkin ring

7" (18cm) of red jumbo rickrack

50" (127cm) of black standard rickrack

70" (178cm) of red baby rickrack

17" (43cm) grosgrain ribbon
printed with roosters

craft glue

¼" (6mm) double-sided craft tape

sewing machine and black,
red and off-white thread

fusible web and iron

clear nail polish

ANOTHER SIMPLY BEAUTIFUL IDEA

**For a great wedding shower
gift, trim an entire set of linens
in the bride's favorite colors.
Don't overlook plain kitchen
towels and quilted potholders.
Both are easily trimmed with
rickrack or grosgrain ribbon.**

Add whimsy to plain table linens with zigzags of inexpensive rickrack. Often overlooked, this versatile trim has recently come back into vogue. Ideal for everyday wear and sturdy enough to withstand regular machine washings, the limited red, black and white color palette unifies the rickrack and grosgrain ribbon pieces so they work together as a set.

one · Thread the sewing machine with black thread and machine stitch the standard sized black rickrack around the entire inside edge of the round place mat. Cut off the unused rickrack and apply clear nail polish to the cut edge to prevent it from unraveling.

two · Thread the sewing machine with red thread and machine stitch a length of red baby rickrack down each side of the black napkin, approximately ¾" (19mm) from the outside edge. The rickrack lengths will cross over one another at each corner. Apply clear nail polish to the cut rickrack ends to prevent them from fraying.

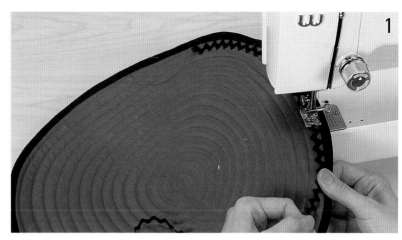

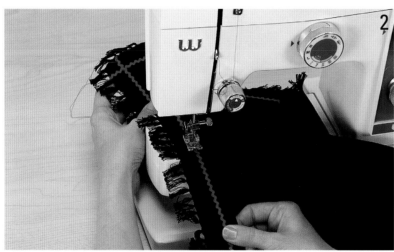

three · Apply a strip of fusible web across one side of the red napkin, ¾" (19mm) from the outside edge. Remove the paper backing and lay the grosgrain ribbon over the web. Tuck the cut ribbon ends under and iron the ribbon in place to activate the fusible web.

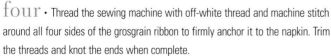

four · Thread the sewing machine with off-white thread and machine stitch around all four sides of the grosgrain ribbon to firmly anchor it to the napkin. Trim the threads and knot the ends when complete.

five · Apply a strip of double-sided craft tape around the center of the napkin ring. Peel off the protective backing and wrap the center of the red jumbo rickrack over the exposed adhesive. Cut off the unused rickrack length and apply nail polish to the cut ends to prevent them from fraying. If necessary, glue the second rickrack end down over the first.

window wreath

MATERIALS

14" (36cm) of 1½" (4cm) wide
wire-edged ribbon

9" (23cm) of ½" (13mm) wide
blue grosgrain ribbon

acrylic crystal beads

pendant crystal bead

blue acrylic crystal bead

two 18" (46cm) pieces of 24-gauge wire

2" (5cm) wire scrap

nail polish

scissors

wire cutters

round-nose pliers

tip > If you prefer real glass, this project is a great way to recycle chandelier crystals. Often they're sold individually at lampshops.

When sunlight streams through the window ornament, the faceted beads will scatter prisms of color into the room. Two-toned silk ribbons not only dress up the finished ornament, they serve as a hanger and disguise the wire connection.

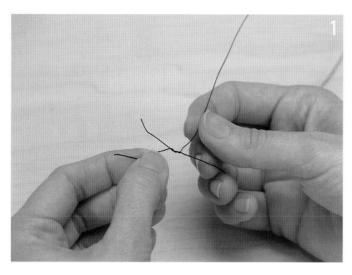

one · Starting 1" (3cm) from the wire ends, twist the ends together three times.

two · Working with the other end of the wires, pass one wire through the base of an acrylic bead and the second wire through the top of the bead. Pull up on both wires to slide the bead down until it rests approximately ½" (13mm) above the twists in the wire.

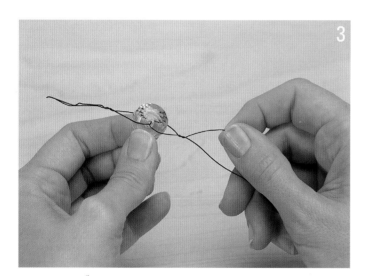

three · Twist the wires together three more times ½" (13mm) above the bead.

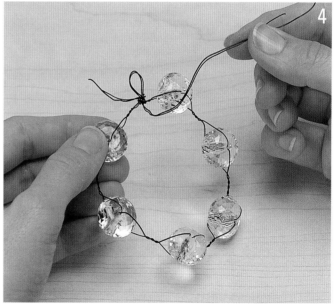

four · Repeat steps 2 and 3 five more times, then wrap the wire ends around the starting wires to shape the beaded wires into a wreath. Form the remaining wire length into a small hanging loop. Use wire cutters to trim the wire ends.

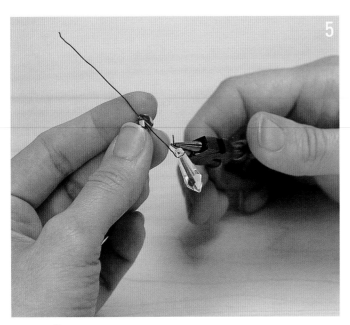

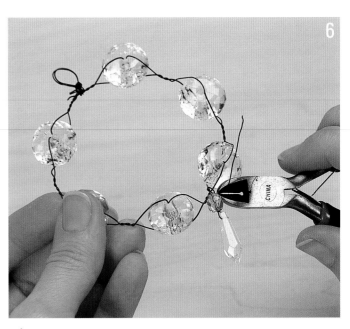

five · Thread a pendant crystal bead followed by a blue crystal bead onto the 2" (5cm) wire scrap. Use round-nose pliers to bend the wire end up around the top of the pendant bead to secure it in place.

six · Loop the other end of the wire around the base of the beaded wreath. Twist the wire end back around itself, then trim away the excess wire.

seven · Thread the ½" (13mm) grosgrain ribbon through the hanging loop. Bring the ends together and tie them in an overhand knot. Trim the ends on the diagonal and apply polish to the cut edges to prevent fraying.

tip > Pick a sunny spot to hang your wreath to enjoy the best light refraction against your floors and walls. Consider an east-facing window to capture the first rays of the morning sun. Simplify the hanging process by lengthening the hanging ribbon so that the wreath can be looped directly over an existing curtain rod.

eight · Tie the 1½" (4cm) wire-edged ribbon in a bow around the base of the hanging loop. Trim the ends straight and then apply polish to the cut edges to prevent fraying.

MORE SIMPLY BEAUTIFUL IDEAS

Experiment with different sized and shaped beads. Each variety will alter the wire wreath shape and size. Use holiday colored ribbon to make a Christmas tree ornament by simply coordinating the colored crystal bead with the new ribbon color.

organgdy flowers

flower stamen (sold with
bridal craft accessories)

three 18" (46cm) 20-gauge floral stems

1½" (4cm) wide wire-edged sheer ribbon

1½" (4cm) wide sheer ribbon

¼" (6mm) wide green satin ribbon

white floral tape

glue gun

BIG FLOWER

set of three 5" (13cm) long
sheer ribbon pieces

two sets of three 7" (18cm) long
sheer ribbon pieces

BUD

two 4" (10cm) ribbon pieces
for unwired loops

one 6" (15cm) ribbon piece
for wired loops

LEAF

7" (18cm) of 1½" (4cm) wide
two-toned green satin ribbon

ANOTHER SIMPLY BEAUTIFUL IDEA

This project lends itself to
experimentation. Try different
colors and varieties of ribbon.
Enlarge or decrease the length
of the ribbons to alter the size
of the petals. More loops will
make a larger flower, and fewer
loops will make a smaller
flower. Regardless of color, size
or shape, the finished bouquet
will be everlasting. When necessary, simply reshape the wired
petal loops with your fingertips.

These quick and easy flowers are made almost entirely out of ribbon. No sewing is required! The simple trick behind this original approach is floral tape. Start with a single blossom, and once you've discovered firsthand how simple the process is, you won't hesitate to assemble an entire ribbon flower bouquet.

big flower

The largest ribbon flowers make the biggest splash of color and require the most ribbon.

one · Twist the wire end of the flower stamen around the top of a green floral stem.

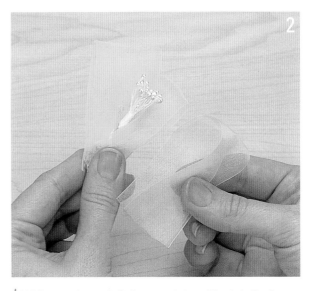

two · Fold three 5" (13cm) lengths of sheer ribbon in half to form petal loops. Place these three loops, cut ends down, around the flower stamen. Tightly wrap floral tape around the loop ends to secure them around the base of the stamen.

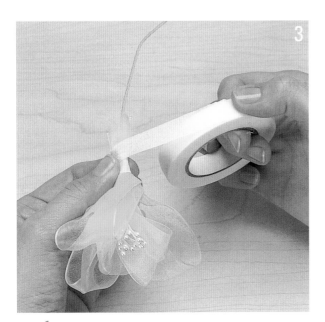

three · Fold three 7" (18cm) lengths of wired sheer ribbon into loops and place them around the loops from step 2. Tightly wrap this second set of loops in place with floral tape.

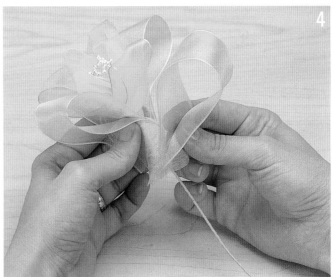

four · Fold three more 7" (18cm) lengths of wired ribbon into petal loops and position them around the flower to finish filling out its shape. Tightly wrap this final set of loops in place (over the loops placed in step 3) with floral tape.

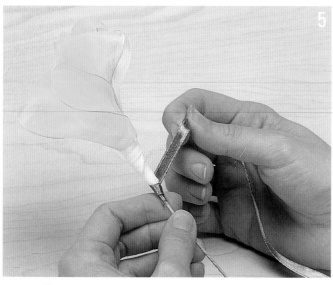

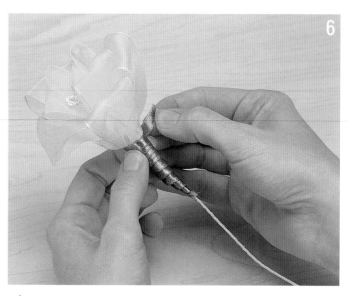

five · Conceal the floral tape with ¼" (6mm) wide green satin ribbon. Spiral it up from the floral stem to just beneath the flower petal loops.

six · Cut the ribbon off the spool and hot glue the end against the wrapped ribbon.

flower bud

Makes a small accent to accompany the big flower. The flower bud doesn't require a flower stamen.

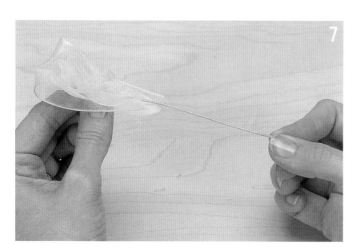

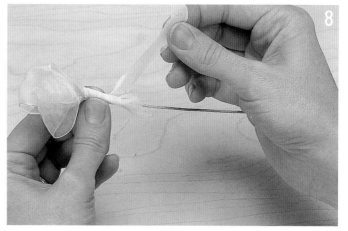

seven · Fold two 4" (10cm) unwired ribbon lengths in half to make petal loops. Position the loops over and around the top of a floral stem to disguise the wire end. Fold a 6" (15cm) wired ribbon length into a petal loop and wrap it around the covered floral wire end so it partially conceals the unwired loop ends.

eight · Tightly wrap all three of the ribbon ends against the floral wire with floral tape.

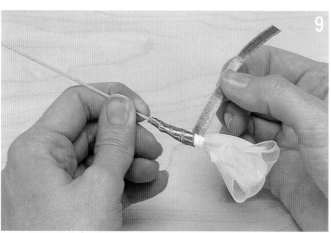

nine · Conceal the floral tape with ¼" (6mm) wide green satin ribbon. Spiral it up from the floral stem to just beneath the bud loops. Secure the end with hot glue.

leaf

Add leaves to either the bud or flower. Without leaves, the floral stem may look unfinished.

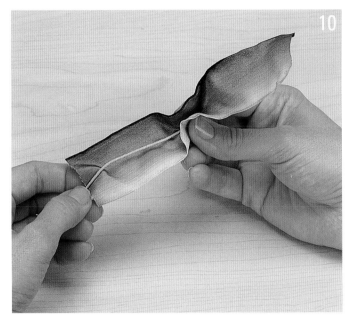

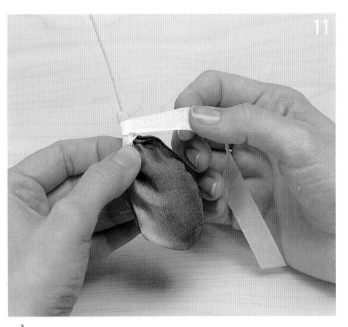

ten · Place the end of a floral stem in the center of a 7" (18cm) length of two-toned ribbon. Pinch the center of the ribbon against the wire and then fold the end of the ribbon down so both ends meet on either side of the wire.

eleven · Use floral tape to tightly gather the ribbon ends around the floral stem. Conceal the floral tape by wrapping it with the ¼" (6mm) green satin ribbon. Trim the floral stem below the leaf so that it's 6" (15cm) long.

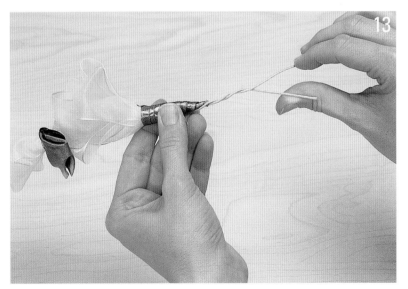

twelve · Connect the finished leaf to the bud by wrapping the leaf stem around the bud stem. If necessary, trim the leaf stems so they fit. Trim the bud stem to 8" (20cm) long.

thirteen · Twist the bud stem onto the flower stem and if necessary, trim the end. Trim the flower stem the appropriate length for your vase.

glass plate

clear glass plate

assorted sheer and organdy ribbons:
½" (13mm) to 2" (5cm) widths

¼" (6mm) wide copper tape

Mod Podge découpage medium

paintbrush

wooden burnishing tool or craft stick

ANOTHER SIMPLY BEAUTIFUL IDEA

Create different looks by using more vibrant colored lightweight ribbons and changing the way they're positioned. Lay all the ribbons in the same direction across the plate or create a haphazard, crisscross pattern.

A clear departure from traditional ribbon crafts, these ribbons have been laminated to glass. Light passes through the plate to illuminate the intricate weaving of sheer ribbons underneath. Whether the finished plate is mounted on a wall or placed on a table, it's sure to attract interest and compliments.

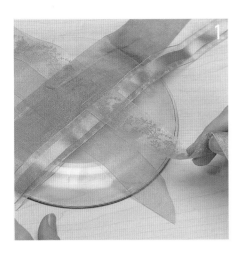

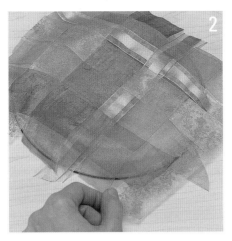

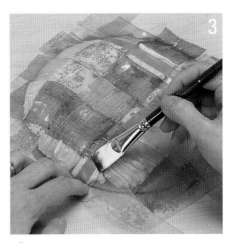

one · Invert the plate over a protected work surface and then brush a layer of découpage medium over the underside. Lay two ribbons vertically down the center of the plate and then weave two more ribbons horizontally through the center of them.

two · Continue weaving additional ribbon lengths around the sides of the initial weaving until the entire underside of the plate is covered. Adjust the ribbons so they lie tightly against one another, eliminating any uncovered glass.

three · Use the brush to gently dab Mod Podge over the ribbons. Be careful not to disturb their placement. Allow the glue to saturate through the ribbon layers to ensure they'll be firmly anchored to the glass after the glue dries.

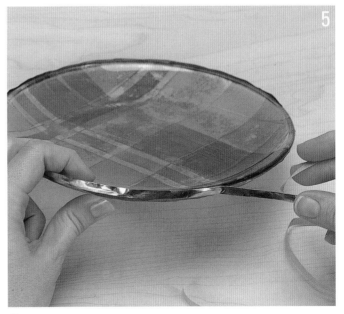

four · Allow the découpage medium to dry overnight. After the plate has completely dried, use scissors to trim away any ribbon that extends beyond the plate rim.

five · Apply copper tape around the plate, covering where the ribbon connects to the glass. Use a burnishing tool to smooth the metal tape edges against the plate.

*tip > The finished plate should not be submerged in water. Use a damp cloth to wipe the surface clean.

special occasions

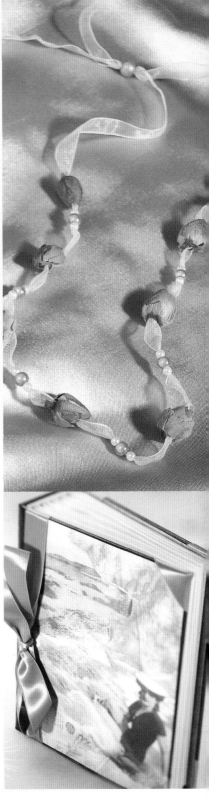

make even the smallest celebration a special occasion with ribbon-inspired crafts. Their satin elegance and timeless beauty will add style to any event any day of the year. In this section you'll find inspiration to make every event a little more special.

Blooming baskets herald spring when they're woven with light green and yellow ribbon and crowned with silk anemones. Ideal for a summertime wedding, the colorful toss-away reception bouquet is adorned with vibrant pink and purple ribbon. Fall fairies dressed in autumn brown and ochre ribbons capture the joy of the harvest season as they hang from a spray of bittersweet. Christmas ornaments wrapped in green and red ribbons take the chill out of winter and add cheer to the evergreen tree.

Regardless of the season, ribbons are an integral part of the wedding decorations. I've added splashes of color to update and personalize my favorite wedding ideas. Pink miracle beads highlight the delicate rosebud necklace. Green ribbon peeks through the ring bearer's pillow that unties to become a useful table linen. Luminous gold vellum is the background for a timeless anniversary card stitched with silk ribbon. These elegant projects will add a personal touch to these once-in-a-lifetime special occasions.

CHAPTER

2

spring spool basket

MATERIALS

3¼" (8cm) cardboard ribbon spool

ten 3" (8cm) bamboo skewers

12" (30cm) of 1½" (4cm) wide
double-sided yellow/green satin ribbon

⅝" (16mm) wide green grosgrain ribbon

15" (38cm) of ⅛" (3mm) pink satin ribbon

pink and yellow anemone silk flowers

scrapbook paper

10mm wood beads

Aleene's 2 in 1 glue

glue gun

⅛" (3mm) hole punch

clear nail polish

NOTE: Grosgrain ribbon width
should match the spool width.

Brimming with flowers, this sunny basket will surely brighten someone's day. It's a clever way to recycle as a cardboard ribbon spool forms the base of the basket. The basket sides are made from cut bamboo skewers. Together they make an easily assembled framework for ribbons and silk flowers. This project is a celebration of spring!

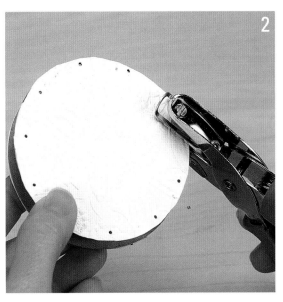

one · Use the spool as your guide to cut two circles from the scrapbook paper. Use paper glue to attach a decorative paper circle over both sides of the spool. If necessary, trim the paper edges.

two · Use a hole punch to create ten holes, 1" (3cm) apart, around the top of the spool. Try to position the holes as far in from the rim as possible to prevent the cardboard from tearing.

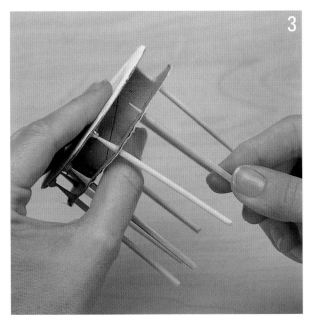

three · Insert a trimmed bamboo skewer, sharp end first, into each hole around the spool. Stabilize the skewer by adding a generous dollop of hot glue to the pointed tip. Hold the skewer upright while the glue sets.

four · Thread a single wood bead onto each skewer spoke.

*tip > When you cut length from the skewer, cut from the flat end and leave the pointed end intact.

five · Weave the 1½" (4cm) wide double-sided satin ribbon in and out through the spokes. Cut off any unused ribbon length and hot glue the loose ribbon ends together.

six · Cut the stems off the silk flowers and pull out the flower centers. Discard the stems and centers but retain five leaves. Thread the center of the silk flower petals down over the top of each spoke. Alternate the pink and yellow petals around the spool.

seven · Cap the spokes one at a time by adding a dot of glue to the end of the bamboo and then sliding a bead into the glue.

eight · Apply hot glue around the outside of the skewers' tips and wrap the ⅝" (16mm) green grosgrain ribbon over the glue to conceal their connection between the rims of the spool. Trim the end of the ribbon, and apply clear nail polish to prevent fraying.

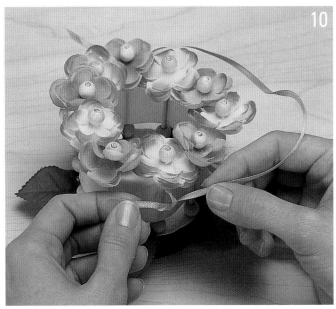

nine · Hot glue a leaf between every other skewer around the base of the basket.

ten · Tie each end of the ⅛" (3mm) pink satin ribbon under a flower on opposite sides of the basket to make the handle.

ANOTHER SIMPLY BEAUTIFUL IDEA

Need more room to pack gifts and goodies? The larger basket starts with a 4" (10cm) cardboard spool that is encircled by seventeen 4" (10cm) high bamboo spokes. The spokes are topped by either yellow, pink or white silk flower petals and capped with pink or white wooden beads. Span the height of the taller spokes by weaving two separate lengths of ribbon through them, one positioned over the other. Encircle the outside edge of the spool with the leaves. Overlap the top and bottom of each leaf so they completely conceal the sides of the spool.

seaside photo album

MATERIALS

photo album

⅞" (22mm) wide double-faced (shiny on both sides) satin ribbon

two coordinated patterned scrapbook papers

½" (13mm) wide double-sided craft tape

Aleene's Memory Glue

NOTE: Use the album as your guide to cut the scrapbook paper for the outside front and back covers and spine. Cut the inside front and back covers from the second type of patterned paper.

ANOTHER SIMPLY BEAUTIFUL IDEA

Use this technique to custom design an album for special photographs. Pair retro baby and toy images with pastel colored ribbon for newborn pictures, and an antique bell, dove, or heart and flower images with white or ivory ribbon for wedding pictures.

Share your vacation snapshots with style. This retro album will keep holiday memories secure. Beautiful scrapbook paper and double-faced satin ribbon conceal the plain covers of an inexpensive photo album and transform them into a treasured keepsake.

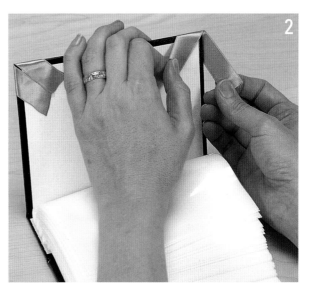

one · Remove the protective plastic covering from the album cover. Glue the cut scrapbook paper over the front, back and spine of the album.

two · Wrap a 5" (13cm) ribbon length around each of the four album corners. Secure the ribbon ends inside the album covers with small diagonal strips of double-sided craft tape.

three · Glue the second set of scrapbook papers over the inside front and back album covers to conceal the ends of the ribbon.

four · Wrap a length of ribbon around the back cover to conceal the connection between the paper coverings and the actual blue album cover. Secure the ribbon ends against the inside back cover with double-sided craft tape.

five · Wrap a second length of ribbon around the underside of the front cover, concealing the paper edge. Bring the ribbon ends together at the center of the front cover and tie them into a generous bow. Trim the ribbon ends and apply nail polish to the cut edges to prevent them from fraying.

fall fairy

MATERIALS

patterns (page 124)

cardstock

three 4½" (11cm) lengths of 1½" (4cm) wide wired yellow ribbon (for inner skirt)

three 4½" (11cm) lengths of 2⅜" (6cm) wide wire-edged golden ribbon (two front, one back outer skirt)

five pieces of ⅝" (16mm) wide wire-edged brown ribbon (three pieces front, two pieces back shirt)

¼" (6mm) sheer burgundy ribbon (for bow)

10" (25cm) of ⅛" (3mm) green ribbon (for hanger)

two feathers

small silk floral leaves

doll hair

bittersweet

fine-tip black pen

colored pencils

glue gun

wire cutters

ANOTHER SIMPLY BEAUTIFUL IDEA

Make a fairy for every season. Look for silk pussy willows for spring, blooming trellis roses for summer and frosted branches for winter. The skin, hair and ribbon colors can easily be coordinated to match the floral selection or your room décor.

Prepare for a flight of fantasy! This charming fairy wall hanging will brighten your décor. Easily assembled over a cardboard pattern, she's brought to life with richly textured ribbons, feathers and doll hair. Always in flight, the finished fairy is suspended from brightly colored bittersweet.

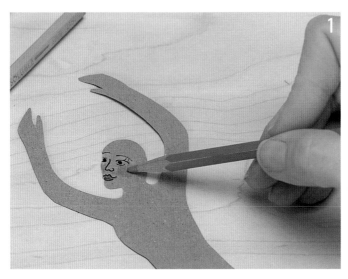

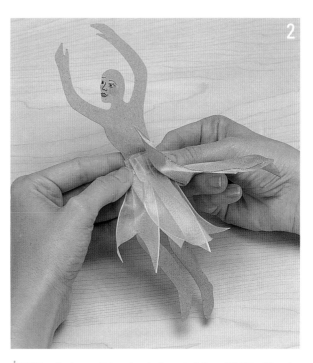

one · Cut the fairy pattern on page 124 from cardstock and draw and outline the features with a fine-tip black pen. Blush the cheeks and fill the lips with red colored pencil, then apply eye shadow with green colored pencil.

two · Cut inverted V notches in the end of three 4½" (11cm) lengths of 1½" (4cm) wide yellow ribbon. Fold the top end of each ribbon in half and hot glue them around the fairy's waist to make the inner skirt. Cut an inverted V notch in the end of two 4½" (11cm) lengths of 2⅜" (6cm) wide wire-edged golden ribbon. Hot glue the top end of the golden ribbons over the yellow ribbons to complete the front of the outer skirt.

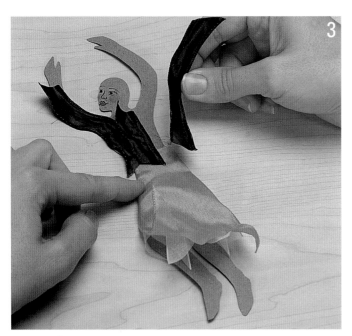

three · The fairy's shirt is made out of three strips of ⅝" (16mm) wide wire-edged brown ribbon. Glue a ribbon length down each arm and position the third ribbon between them. Cut the ends of each ribbon at an angle.

four · To make shoes, fold two small, brown ribbon scraps lengthwise and glue them around the bottom of each foot.

tip > You may want to stamp your fairy's face rather than draw it. There are some excellent face stamps on the market, and this would be a good excuse to visit your local stamp store.

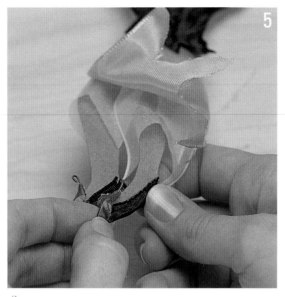

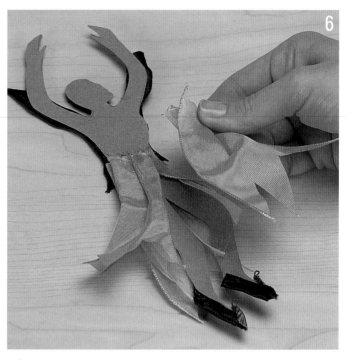

five · Decorate the top of each shoe with a small silk floral leaf. Trim the excess wire and hot glue the leaf in place.

six · Turn the fairy over and glue the tops of two notched 4½" (11cm) lengths of 2⅜" (6cm) wide golden wire-edged ribbon to the back of the fairy's waist to make the back of the outer skirt.

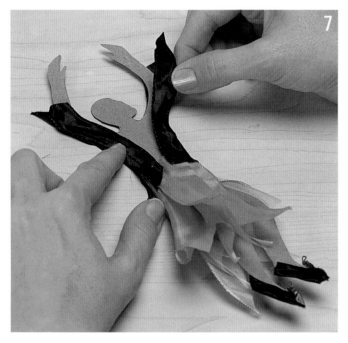

seven · Complete the back of the fairy's shirt with two strips of ⅝" (16mm) wide brown wire-edged ribbon. Hot glue a ribbon down each of the fairy's arms and then cut the ribbon ends at an angle.

eight · Hot glue two feathers to the center of the fairy's back to make her wings.

nine · Turn the fairy right side up, then hot glue a generous amount of doll hair to the top of her head.

ten · Fold the fairy's hands around the bittersweet, then hot glue them in place.

eleven · Loop the ⅛" (3mm) wide green hanging ribbon around the top of the bittersweet. Bring the ends together and tie them in an overhand knot. Tie the ¼" (6mm) burgundy ribbon in a small bow. Trim the ends and hot glue it to the front of the fairy's shirt.

*tip > Do you know someone who is crazy about fairies? Reduce the size of the pattern to make them a gift set of fairy notecards. Or consider mounting a finished fairy onto a blank diary or a photo album.

petal ornaments

8½" (22cm) Styrofoam ball

½" (13mm) of 1½" (4cm) wide green organdy leaf ribbon

12" (30cm) of ⅛" (3mm) wide green satin ribbon (hanger)

13" (33cm) of 1½" (4cm) wide sheer organdy ribbon

pearl bead

red silk flowers (such as geraniums and poinsettias)

Hold the Foam glue

two corsage pins

wire cutters

ANOTHER SIMPLY BEAUTIFUL IDEA

Silk gardenia flowers make a beautiful white version of this ornament that is fitting for both Christmas and weddings. Consider modifying this technique to make bigger hanging petal balls for wedding decorations. Start with a large Styrofoam ball. Wrap two lengths of leaf ribbon around the ball, intersecting at the top and bottom. Purchase additional silk flowers to cover the increased surface.

Specialty organdy ribbon stitched with pressed silk leaves was the inspiration behind this design. The wide ribbon beautifully covers the Styrofoam ball, and the exposed Styrofoam sides are concealed with red flower petals. Two pearl corsage pin flower centers are the final decorative touch. This blooming ornament adds a splash of vibrant color to the Christmas tree.

one · Tie the ⅛" (3mm) wide green satin ribbon around the center of the leaf ribbon. The satin ribbon will become the ornament hanger.

two · Apply a line of Hold the Foam glue around the ball and wrap the leaf ribbon over the glue. Add more glue to the ribbon ends to secure them against the bottom of the ornament. The hanging ribbon should be positioned at the top of the ball.

three · Remove the stems and flower centers from the silk flowers. Working on one side of the ornament, add more glue to the center of the uncovered Styrofoam. Press two silk flower petal rings into the glue. Use wire cutters to shorten the end of the corsage pin. Pierce the shortened pin into the center of the silk petals.

four · Continue adding glue and flower petals around the central flower until all the Styrofoam is covered. Repeat steps 3 and 4 to add a flower and petals to the other side of the ornament.

five · Bring the satin hanging ribbon ends together and tie the organdy ribbon in a bow around the bottom of them. Slide a pearl bead onto the ends of the hanging ribbon. Tie the ends of the hanging ribbon together in an overhand knot.

buttoned baubles

MATERIALS

3½" (9cm) diameter clear glass ornament

11½" (29cm) of 1" (3cm) wide
grosgrain ivory ribbon
(to encircle the glass ornament)

11½" (29cm) of ½" (13mm) wide
red and white gingham ribbon
(to encircle the glass ornament)

¼" (6mm) wide red and ivory satin ribbon

Assorted red, green and white buttons
[¼" to ½" (6mm to 13mm) in diameter]

large ivory button

½" (13mm) wide double-sided craft tape

sewing needle and white thread

clear nail polish

ANOTHER SIMPLY
BEAUTIFUL
IDEA

T rim your tree with these classic ornaments. Ribbon adds a homespun touch to lightweight glass balls. Craft tape holds the wrapped ribbon in place, and the metal ornament top is replaced with a large button to keep the design simple.

This ornament uses two lengths of red gingham ribbons. Cross the center of a vertical ribbon over a horizontal ribbon and stitch a button through the overlap. Wrap two pieces of tape around the glass ball. Position the button over the crossed tape, and press the four ribbon ends over the exposed adhesive. Thread the metal hanger through a large green button. Tie an ivory ribbon around one side of the hanger, and loop a red hanging ribbon through the hanger.

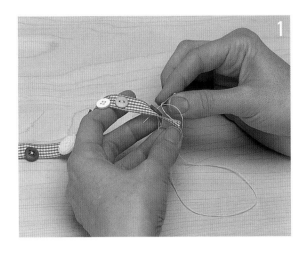

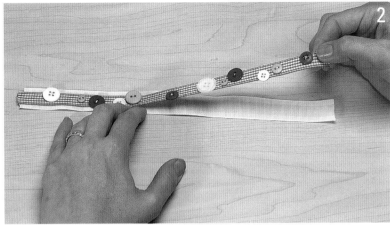

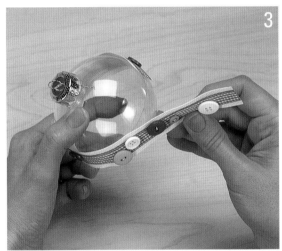

one · Sew a variety of red, green and white buttons along the gingham ribbon. Alternate the colors and randomly position the buttons along the ribbon length.

two · Apply a strip of double-sided craft tape down the center of the grosgrain ribbon. Peel off the backing and lay the gingham ribbon over the center of the grosgrain ribbon. Firmly press the gingham ribbon into the grosgrain ribbon.

three · Apply double-sided craft tape around the center of the glass ornament. Peel off the backing and wrap the grosgrain ribbon around the adhesive. Trim the end of the ribbons and apply clear nail polish to the cut edge to prevent them from fraying.

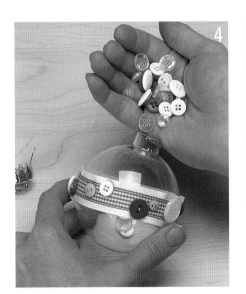

four · Remove the metal ornament top. Pull out the wire hanger. Save it for the next step and discard the metal cap. Pour a mixture of small red, green and white buttons into the top opening.

five · Thread the two wire ends of the hanger through a pair of buttonholes in a large ivory button. Reinsert the wire ends into the top of the glass ornament. The button should cover the top of the glass opening.

six · Tie a ¼" (6mm) wide red ribbon through one side of the wire hanger and tie the ribbon in a bow. For the hanging ribbon, loop a ¼" (6mm) wide ivory ribbon through the hanger. Bring the ends together and tie them in an overhand knot.

dragonfly card

MATERIALS

4" x 5½" (10cm x 14cm) white cardstock card

1⅜" x 5½" (3cm x 14cm) purple scrapbook paper strip

5½" (14cm) of ⅝" (16mm) wide yellow ribbon

four 1" (3cm) lengths of ⅛" (3mm) wide white ribbon (for wings)

five rhinestones (two small round, one larger round, one larger pointed oval and one smaller pointed oval)

double-sided craft tape

embellishment glue

paper glue

tip > You can vary the design of the dragonfly if you can't find the same rhinestones used here. You can find small metal dragonfly embellishments, or combine different varieties of rhinestones to achieve the same effect.

Shimmering satin ribbon makes this note card simply elegant. Achieve the limited color palette by coordinating the ribbon and rhinestones to the printed paper strip. Send a single card to brighten someone's day or consider making a set in different color schemes to present as a gift.

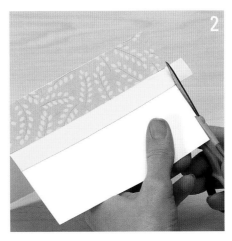

one · Use paper glue to mount the purple paper strip to the front of the card. Line the left edge of the paper strip against the folded edge of the card.

two · Use double-sided craft tape to attach the yellow ribbon against the bottom edge of the paper strip. Trim the sides of the ribbon so it's even with the side of the card.

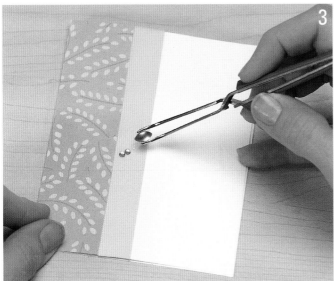

three · Use embellishment glue to position two small round rhinestones over the center of the yellow ribbon to make the end of the dragonfly's tail. Add a larger pointed oval rhinestone to the top of the tail. This will become the abdomen.

four · Use more embellishment glue to attach two pairs of 1" (3cm) long ⅛" (3mm) wide ribbon dragonfly wings. Glue one end of each pair of wings above the oval rhinestone so that the ribbon extends out from either side of the dragonfly.

five · Glue the large round rhinestone body over the glued wing ends. Finish by gluing the small pointed oval head across the top of the body.

flower card

MATERIALS

4¼" x 5½" (11cm x 14cm) green card-stock note card and envelope

6½" (17cm) long ½" (13mm) wide red and white gingham ribbon

4" (10cm) long ⅛" (3mm) wide black ribbon with white polka dots

1½" (4cm) long ¼" (6mm) wide green satin ribbon

1⅛" (3cm) by 4" (10cm) patterned scrapbook paper

¼" (6mm) button

paper glue

sewing needle and white thread

glue gun

tip > For an anniversary, add formality by assembling the flower over a metallic silver or gold card and switch to solid colored satin ribbons. To completely change the sentiment, select different scrapbook papers and ribbon colors. To celebrate a newborn's arrival, look for yellow, pink, or light blue baby paper and pair it with pastel colored ribbon.

This cheery little handmade card makes a perfect, unexpected love note. A single flower sprouts from a scrapbook paper flowerbed. Perpetually blooming, this ruffled blossom will never fade or wither.

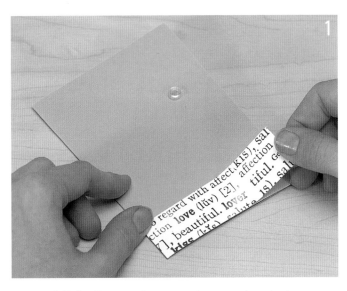

one · Use paper glue to mount the patterned scrapbook paper across the base of the note card.

two · Hot glue the button to the right side of the card, a third of the way down from the top. Stitch down one side of the gingham ribbon length with needle and thread. Ruffle the stitched ribbon (see page 13). Wrap the ruffled ribbon around the button. If necessary, adjust the ruffling before tying the thread ends together in a knot. Trim away the excess thread and apply a couple of dots of hot glue under the ruffled flower to help anchor the ribbon to the card.

three · Tuck one end of the polka dot ribbon stem under the base of the ruffled flower. Glue the length of the stem straight down to the base of the card. Cut the ribbon so that it is flush with the base of the card.

four · Before the stem is firmly set in place, fold the satin ribbon in half to make a leaf. Glue the ribbon ends together and tuck them under the stem.

fashion purse card

MATERIALS

pattern (see page 124)

3½" (9cm) length of ⅛" (3mm) wide black satin ribbon (for handle)

2" (5cm) of ⅝" (16mm) wide pink feather-edged ribbon

pink ribbon rose

4¼" x 5½" (11cm x 14cm) silver cardstock note cards and envelope

4¼" x 5½" (11cm x 14cm) black and white checkered scrapbook paper

black and silver paper scraps

paper glue

embellishment glue

double-sided craft tape

tip > If you're in a hurry, substitute hot glue for the embellishment glue on the cards. It will quickly anchor the ribbon rose to the purse and the tied bows to the fashion shoes card.

Pretty in pink! This little rosebud purse is the perfect note card to send to fashion-loving girlfriends. Send this card as an invitation for a girl's-only afternoon of lunch and shopping.

one · Cut the purse from black and silver paper using the pattern on page 124. Use paper glue to mount the purse just below the center front of the silver note card. Fold the ⅛" (3mm) wide ribbon length in half to make the purse handle. Use embellishment glue to attach the handle ends just above the top of the purse.

two · Use double-sided craft tape to attach the pink feather-edged ribbon over the handle ends and the top of the purse.

three · Use more embellishment glue to attach a single ribbon rose to the center of the pink ribbon. Allow the glue to dry completely before sending the card.

four · Slip a rectangle of black and white patterned scrapbook paper inside the purchased envelope. Once you've checked the fit, glue it in place with paper glue. The customized envelope will complement the finished purse card.

fashion shoes card

MATERIALS

patterns (page 124)

⅛" (3mm) wide black ribbon

3" x 4½" (8cm x 11cm) pink
and white scrapbook paper

4¼" x 5½" (11cm x 14cm) ivory
cardstock note card and envelope

black paper scraps

checkered paper scraps

paper glue

embellishment glue

ANOTHER SIMPLY BEAUTIFUL IDEA

Dress up purchased cards with small, tied ribbon bows. Add a bow to the stems of a flower bouquet or around the waist of a wedding dress.

Ooh la la! Très chic. These little black shoes will match almost any personal sentiment. It's an especially fitting card to send to someone who can never resist a new pair of shoes!

one · Use paper glue to mount pink and white scrapbook paper over the center front of the ivory card.

two · Cut the larger shoe pattern (on page 124) out of a black paper scrap, then cut the smaller shoe inserts out of checkered scraps. Use paper glue to mount the checkered inserts inside the black shoes.

three · Glue the shoes over the center of the pink and white scrapbook paper.

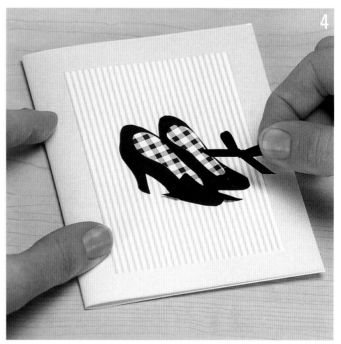

four · Tie a single length of ribbon into a small bow. Adjust the loops and trim the ends so that it will fit over the toe of a shoe. Make a matching bow with a second length of ribbon. Use embellishment glue to attach a bow to the end of each checkered insert. Let the glue dry completely before mailing.

wedding card

MATERIALS

5" x 6½" (13cm x 17cm) window card [window: 2½" x 4" (6cm x 10cm)]

silk embroidery ribbon

heart sticker (Mrs. Grossman's)

4½" x 6¼" (11cm x 16cm) gold vellum sheet

double-sided craft tape

sewing needle (with an eye large enough to accommodate the ribbon)

awl

tip > Display the finished card by a light source to illuminate the semitranslucent vellum window.

Lightweight silk ribbon beautifully accents this simple sticker card. Coordinate the vellum color to match the occasion. Use ivory for wedding congratulations, pink for Valentine wishes, silver for a twenty-fifth wedding anniversary and gold for a fiftieth anniversary.

one · Open the card and apply double-sided craft tape around the outside edge of the window opening. Mount the gold vellum paper inside the card so it covers the window.

two · Close the card and apply the heart sticker to the vellum so it's centered over the window.

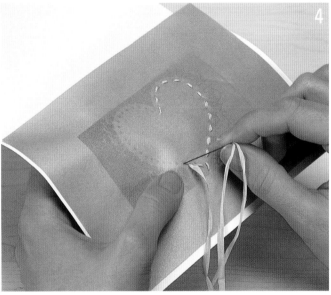

three · Thread the needle with silk ribbon (see page 68). Begin stitching at the center top of the heart sticker, letting a few inches of the ribbon end hang down the front of the heart. Make stitches between the holes in the sticker's decorative edge.

four · Continue stitching around the heart, if necessary use an awl to prepunch holes through the card and vellum before using the needle to stitch the ribbon.

five · Once you've made stitches around the entire heart, tie the ribbon ends into a bow.

rosebud necklace

MATERIALS

33" (84cm) of ¼" (6mm) wide sheer
organdy ribbon

dried rosebuds

6mm Miracle beads

pearl beads

sewing needle (with an eye large enough
to accommodate the ribbon and sharp
enough to pierce the flowers)

tip > To sew with ribbon, start with a supple ribbon with a width compatible to the opening in the eye of the needle. Avoid wire-edged ribbon. Cut the ribbon on the diagonal and pass it through the small opening. Grasp the tip of the ribbon once it passes through the needle hole and pull. You can also use the needle to thread beads on a ribbon.

This necklace brings natural rosebuds, beads and translucent ribbon together to make a delicate keepsake. It's a perfect necklace for a flower girl to wear at a wedding, or a thoughtful handmade gift to give friends and bridesmaids. Whether it's worn or kept in a lingerie drawer, it's a beautiful way to preserve and share the sweet summer scent of garden roses.

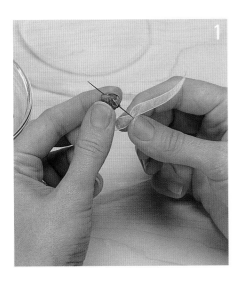
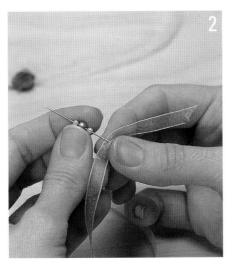

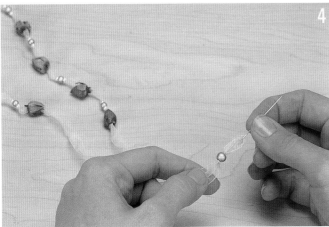

one · Thread the needle with ribbon (see tip page 68). Pierce the needle through the base of a dried rosebud and then draw the needle tip through the bud. Gently slide the rosebud down the ribbon.

two · String the following bead sequence onto the ribbon: one pearl bead, one 6mm Miracle bead and one pearl bead. String a rosebud on the ribbon as you did in step 1. Continue adding the bead sequence then a rosebud six more times. Space the rosebud and the bead sequence ¼" to ½" (6mm to 13mm) apart across the ribbon length.

three · String a final rosebud onto the ribbon and position it ¼" to ½" (6mm to 13mm) from the last sequence.

four · Bring both ribbon ends together and thread them through the eye of the needle. Thread the needle through a 6mm miracle bead.

five · Separate the ribbons and thread a single pearl onto each ribbon end. Tie the ribbon ends in an overhand knot to prevent the beads from falling off. The 6mm Miracle bead will act like a clasp. Slide it up to the small pearl beads to enlarge the necklace to fit over your head, then slide it down toward the rosebuds to shorten the necklace to the desired length.

tip > Dried rosebuds are surprisingly inexpensive. They are packaged in cellophane bags where everlasting naturals are sold. Dried flowers have inherent variations in size, shape and color, so select compact buds with good coloration to string onto your necklace.

ring pillow

20" x 13¼" (51cm x 34cm)
wide tea towel

1 yard (1m) of 1½" (4cm)
wide jacquard ribbon

13" (33cm) of 2" (5cm) wide
green satin ribbon

two 10" (25cm) lengths of
⅛" (3mm) wide white organdy ribbon

rings

polyester fiberfill

nail polish

tip > If you have trouble locating a tea towel, embroidered place mats and dinner napkins are good alternatives. Ask relatives if they have linens stashed away, or check the selection of heirloom linens at specialty antique stores.

This no-sew ring pillow unfolds into a useful table linen after the wedding. The embroidered cutwork subtly reveals a wide satin ribbon that's customized to match your wedding colors. The beautiful jacquard ribbon keeps the rings safely tied to the pillow even if the ring bearer's fingers unexpectedly lose their grip.

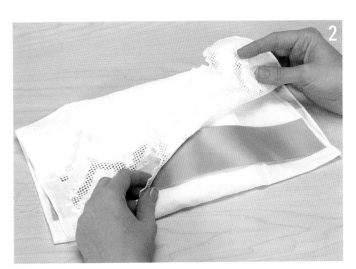

one · Place enough fiberfill in the center of the tea towel to create a pillow. Bring the bottom edge of the towel over the fiberfill and the top decorative edge of the towel down so it lays over the bottom edge.

two · Slide the 2" (5cm) wide green ribbon under the decorative edge of the towel so it can be seen through the openings in the cutwork.

three · Fold both the right and left unpadded sides of the towel under to make a square shaped pillow. Working on the underside of the pillow, connect the side edges together with the ⅛" (3mm) wide organdy ribbon lengths. Thread each end of the first ribbon through openings in the cutwork and then tie the ribbon ends together in a bow. Repeat the process with the second ribbon, positioning it 1" (3cm) from the first bow. Both ribbons should easily untie after the ceremony.

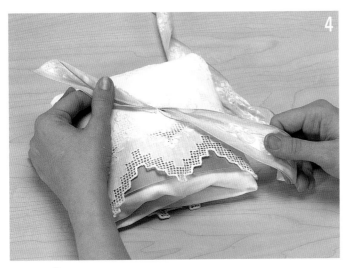

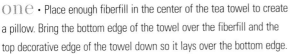

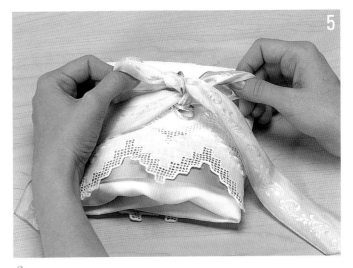

four · Flip the pillow over and thread the 1½" (4cm) wide jacquard ribbon through a cutwork opening on the front of the tea towel.

five · Thread both rings onto one side of the jacquard ribbon, and then tie the ribbon ends in a bow. Make fresh diagonal cuts across the bow ends and apply clear nail polish to prevent them from unraveling.

reception bouquet

MATERIALS

assorted silk florals such as poppies,
gerbera daisies and anemones

2 yards (2m) of ½" (13mm)
pink wire-edged ribbon

1 yard (1m) of ½" (13mm)
purple wire-edge ribbon

2 yards (2m) of 2⅜" (6cm)
purple wire-edged ribbon

assorted berries

white floral tape

clear nail polish

corsage pins

wire cutters

tip > If selecting an assortment of flowers for a bouquet is intimidating, look for manufactured mixed silk flower bouquets that eliminate the guess-work. Cut the bouquet apart and follow the steps to tightly wrap the individual flower stems together.

This eye-catching bouquet is perfect for a bride who wants to add bright color to her wedding reception. Assembled with vibrant silk flowers, the stems are beautifully concealed under richly hued wire ribbon. Whoever catches it will be rewarded with a long-lasting bouquet that can be beautifully displayed in a vase.

one • Before arranging the flowers, cut the leaves from the stems. Assemble the flowers into a bouquet. Group the largest flower varieties at the base and allow the smaller varieties to trail out the top. Try to evenly distribute the different colors and flower varieties. Tightly wrap the stems together with floral tape.

two • Cut the bottoms of the stems at an angle so that the trimmed stems are the same length. Position the center of the ½" (13mm) wide pink wire-edged ribbon around the base of the floral tape. Crisscross the ribbons over the floral tape, working your way up to the base of the flowers. Tie both ribbons in a knot at the top of the wrapped tape.

three • Spiral the ½" (13mm) wide purple wire-edged ribbon up the stems as you did the pink wire-edged ribbon in step 2. This time start wrapping halfway up the pink ribbon and tie the ends of the purple ribbon together in a knot alongside the knotted pink ribbon.

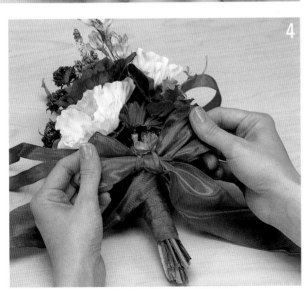

four • Wrap the center of the 2⅜" (6cm) purple wire-edged ribbon above the other ribbons. Tie the 2⅜" (6cm) ribbon ends into a large bow.

five • To make a double bow, fold a ribbon end into a loop behind one side of the bow. Use a corsage pin to anchor the loop in place. Make a second loop with the other end of the ribbon behind the other side of the bow and anchor it in place. Cut an inverted V notch in each ribbon end, and apply clear nail polish to the cut ends to prevent them from fraying.

gifts for family & friends

they're not just for wrapping— luxurious ribbon can be crafted into a beautiful and useful gifts the recipient will treasure forever. Richly colored, textured or patterned ribbon adds impact to otherwise plain, everyday accessories to make an ordinary gift absolutely extraordinary.

Nothing is more precious than a new baby. In this section you'll find irresistible baby gifts and useful accessories. Outfit the little angel in the softness of a rose-edged onesie with matching socks. A looped fleece blanket is perfectly sized to fit in the stroller and keep baby warm. The handy loops hold a rattle within baby's reach, and in a pinch it can be laid across the floor for baby to stretch out. The baby doorknob hanger is an original shower gift topper and subtle reminder to keep the hallways quiet while baby sleeps. The stitched photo sleeves are a beautiful way to announce baby's birth or share your favorite snapshots of her first year.

For newlyweds or friends on the go, there are practical ribbon gifts to accompany any journey. Wrap patterned ribbon around a journal to create a special place to record travels. Sew ribbon to leather or fabric to make a portable travel sketchbook and an easy-to-use cosmetic travel case. Instantly iron layers of ribbon together to make a tailored bookmark or iron them onto an inexpensive drawstring bag to make elegant scented sachets.

All the gifts in this section are easy to customize. Select ribbons that coordinate with friend's and family's personal taste to make thoughtful gifts that will be remembered forever.

CHAPTER

3

baby photo sleeves

MATERIALS

white cardstock

12½" (32cm) of 1½" (4cm) wide organdy ribbon with satin edges

8" (20cm) of ⅜" (10mm) wide plaid ribbon

blue and white patterned scrapbook paper

sticker (rocking horse)

scrapbook glue

clear nail polish

⅛" (3mm) hole punch

sewing machine and blue thread

pinking shears

computer and printer

NOTE: Measurements are for a 3½" x 5" (9cm x 13cm) snapshot. Reduce or enlarge to accommodate larger or smaller photographs.

ANOTHER SIMPLY BEAUTIFUL IDEA

Here's a charming way to share your favorite baby photographs with friends and family. The protective envelope also doubles as a decorative keepsake that can be easily mounted onto a scrapbook page.

For portrait photos, orient the sleeve vertically. You may also consider adapting this project to make an unique birth announcement. Switch the word "Photo" to "Welcome" or "It's a boy/girl!" and then position the baby's name, birthdate and weight on the backside of the sleeve.

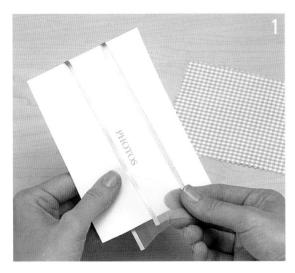

one · Use a computer to print the word *PHOTOS* onto white cardstock. Trim the paper to 4" x 5¾" (10cm x 15cm). Be sure the words are centered between the top and bottom of the trimmed cardstock. Wrap the organdy ribbon around the center of the cardstock. Bring the ends together at the right edge.

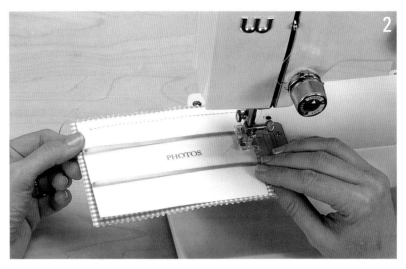

two · Use pinking shears to trim three sides of the scrapbook paper, leaving the left edge straight. The finished rectangle should measure 4½" x 6" (11cm x 15cm). Layer the beribboned cardstock over the scrapbook paper, and machine stitch along the top, right and bottom edges of the layered papers. Trap the ribbon ends while stitching the right edge. Leave the left edge open to insert a photo.

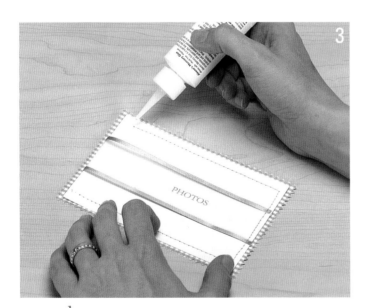

three · Trim the organdy ribbon ends below the seam. Apply a dot of glue to the last stitches on either side of the opening to prevent the stitching from unraveling.

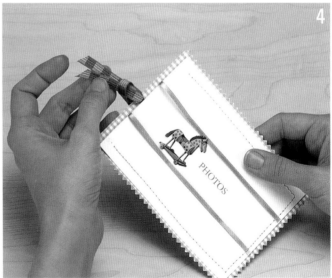

four · Apply a sticker over the ribbon and beside the type. Punch a hole in the left edge of the scrapbook paper. Loop the plaid ribbon through the hole, then trim the ends on the diagonal and apply clear nail polish to prevent fraying.

baby mobile

MATERIALS

craft foam sheets: white, red and black

two ½" (13mm) buttons

patterns (page 125)

three 8" (20cm) lengths of red with white polka dots ribbon, ⅜" (10mm) wide

three 11" (28cm) lengths of black with white polka dots ribbon, ⅜" (10mm) wide

black and white ½" (13mm) wide gingham: 8"(20cm), 9½"(24cm) and 11"(28cm) lengths

red and white ½" (13mm) wide gingham: 8"(20cm), 9½"(24cm) and 11"(28cm) lengths

42" (107cm) of ⅛" (3mm) wide black ribbon (for hanger)

craft foam glue

craft foam bead

sewing needle and black thread

darning needle

tip > This mobile is not an infant toy. It has small parts. Use only with careful supervision and keep out of reach of children under three years of age.

High-contrast red, white and black colors in striking patterns have been proven to engage newborn babies. The sun's ribbon rays will flutter over baby's infant seat or crib, providing captivating visual entertainment during the first few months of baby's infancy.

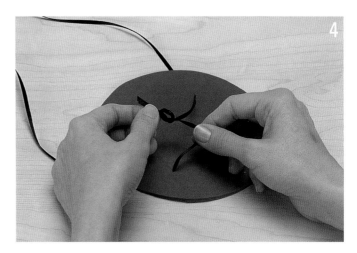

one · Cut out the black, red and white craft foam pieces (see patterns on page 125). Hand sew two red button eyes 2¼" (6cm) from the top of the white foam face, positioning them about ½" (13mm) apart. Use craft foam glue to attach the black foam facial features around the button eyes.

two · Apply craft foam glue to the center of the black foam sun. Place the finished face over the glue and in the center of the sun.

three · Lay the sun facedown with the black side up. Begin gluing the ribbon rays between each point of the sun. Alternate polka dot ribbons with gingham ribbons. Fold up and glue the ends of the polka dot ribbons together to form loops.

four · Thread the darning needle with ⅛" (3mm) wide black ribbon. Make a giant stitch through the center of the red foam circle. Position the needle holes 1¼" (3cm) from each edge. Knot the ends together under the foam circle.

five · Glue the red foam, with the knot side down, over the back of the sun. Slide a craft foam bead over the loop end of the hanging ribbon. Allow the glue to dry completely before use.

*tip > Place heavy books over the finished sun to press the layers firmly together while the glue dries.

baby door hanger

MATERIALS

empty ribbon spool

18" (46cm) of ½" (13mm) wide
woven ribbon [cotton]

16" (41cm) of baby rickrack

18" (46cm) of ½" (13mm) wide
jacquard ribbon

lowercase alphabet scrapbook stickers

pink, blue and white lined
scrapbook paper

two 1" (3cm) lavender pom-poms

paper glue or glue gun

nail polish

Shh…This subtle reminder will help keep the household quiet while baby sleeps. A novel way to recycle a cardboard ribbon spool, the finished lightweight hanger won't bang against the closing door.

ANOTHER SIMPLY BEAUTIFUL IDEA

Customize the colored paper to match the baby's room décor and personalize the message to suit the household. These hangers also make a great topper for wrapped baby shower gifts.

one • Use the ribbon spool as a guide to cut two circles out of the scrapbook paper. Orient the lined pattern horizontally and apply scrapbook stickers along the center of each circle. Use paper glue to mount a circle on each side of the spool.

two • Apply hot glue around the inside rim of the spool. Wrap the center of the rickrack over the glue at the top of the spool. Continue pressing the rickrack into the glue down both sides of the spool. Allow the rickrack ends to hang below the base of the spool.

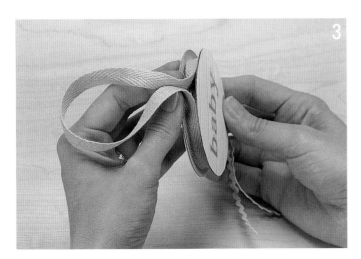

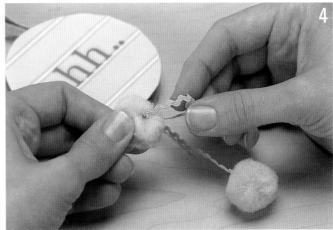

three • Starting at the base of the spool, glue the ends of the woven ribbon over either side of the glued rickrack. Continue hot gluing the woven ribbon up both sides of the spool. The remaining ribbon length will make a loop above the top of the spool.

four • Push aside the fluff to expose the center of the pom-pom, then hot glue the rickrack end to the center of the pom-pom. Pinch the fluff over the glued end to conceal the connection. Attach the second pom-pom to the other rickrack end.

five • Tie the jacquard ribbon in a bow around the base of the woven ribbon loop. Trim the ends on the diagonal and then apply clear nail polish to the cut edge to prevent fraying.

tip > This is not a baby toy. Please keep out of the reach of young children.

onesies

MATERIALS

onesie (3–6 months)

infant socks

17" to 18" (43cm–46cm) pink flower trim

clear nail polish

sewing needle and white thread

A simple addition of flower trim transforms basic baby clothing into wardrobe favorites. Consider making a complete gift set by adding matching trim to a blanket. Tie all the pieces together with coordinating ribbon.

ANOTHER SIMPLY
BEAUTIFUL
IDEA

White trim is a better choice when making the gift before baby's arrival and you're not sure if you'll be celebrating a baby boy or girl.

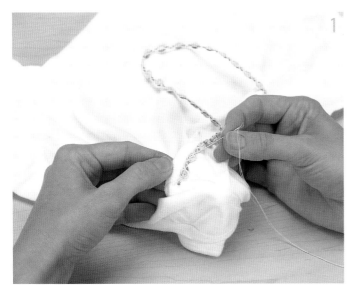

one · Open the boatneck collar at the shoulder seam and begin stitching the trim just below the ribbed edging. Make several stitches around the trim end to help prevent it from unraveling.

two · Continue stitching the trim around the neckline. Be careful to make evenly spaced stitches so the trim lies flat and the undershirt fabric doesn't pucker.

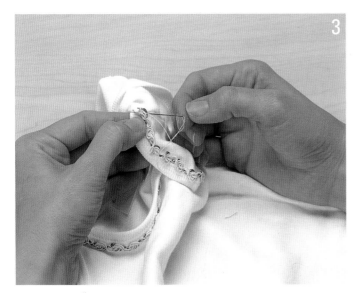

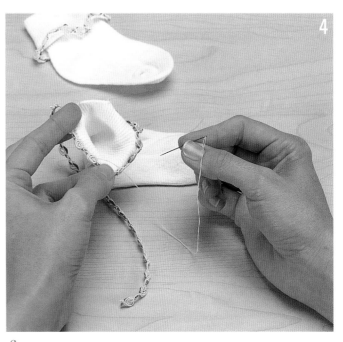

three · Finish stitching the trim to the opposite shoulder. Cut away any excess trim length and make several stitches around the end to prevent it from unraveling. Before folding the open collar back down, apply a dot of nail polish to both trim ends.

four · Use the same technique to stitch the trim to sock cuffs. Stretch the sock cuff between your fingertips or insert a rubber ball into the cuff as you sew. This will ensure that you attach a generous circle of trim. The trim isn't elastic and the added length will allow baby's foot to slide easily in and out of the sock.

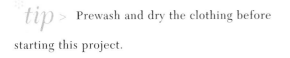

tip > Prewash and dry the clothing before starting this project.

beribboned blanket

MATERIALS

two pieces of 30" (76cm) square
fleece (pink and mint green)

5" (13cm) lengths of ⅞" (2mm)
wide jacquard ribbons in both
white/green and yellow/green

two 5" (13cm) lengths of ¾" (19mm)
wide satin ribbons in yellow and green

5" (13cm) length of ¾" (19mm)
wide feather-edged ribbon in pink

straight pins

sewing machine

sewing needle and thread

tip > This project
is ideal for making use
of ribbon scraps or sale
bin finds. Bag the ribbons
together and bring them
to the fabric store to select
a playful fleece pattern
that will work with them.

This soft snuggly blanket is the perfect size for traveling. It fits easily in the stroller or over a car seat, and in a pinch will lay over carpeting to provide a safe mat for baby to stretch out. The silky loops are fun for baby's fingers to explore and with the help of plastic links will keep toys within reach.

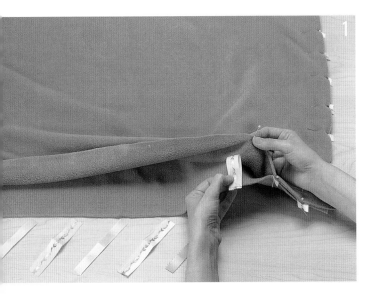

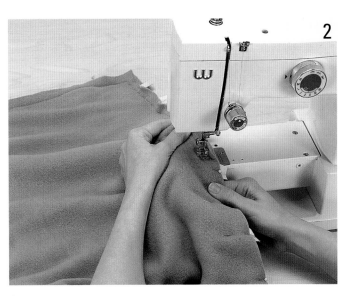

one • Lay the green fleece square over the pink fleece square. Fold a ribbon length in half and place it, loop side first, between the fleece layers, pinning it in place. The ribbon's ends should extend ½" (13mm) beyond the fleece edge. Continue pinning folded ribbons around all four sides of the blanket, spacing them 2" (5cm) apart and alternating the jacquard ribbons with the solid colored satin and feather-edged ribbons.

two • Machine stitch around the edge of the blanket. Remove straight pins as you approach each ribbon loop. Leave a 6" (15cm) opening in the edge to turn the fabric right side out.

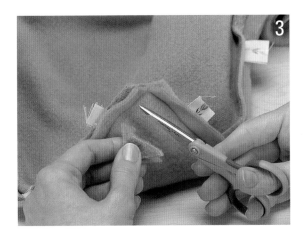

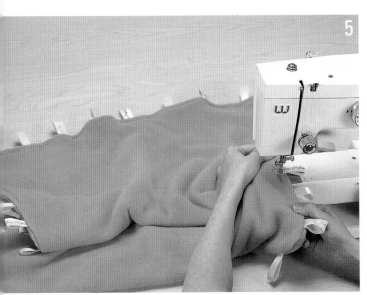

three • Make a small diagonal cut at each corner to remove excess fleece. This will help square the corners. Reach inside the opening to pull the blanket right side out.

four • With needle and thread, hand stitch the opening closed. To maintain the continuous pattern along the blanket edge, be sure to sew through any ribbon loop ends that should be inserted into the opening.

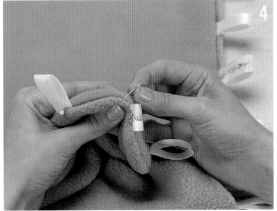

five • To reinforce the ribbon connections, machine stitch a final top stitch seam around the blanket edge.

tip > For a pretty gift, fold the blanket in half, roll it up and tie it closed with the wide jacquard ribbon.

blooming lunch pail

MATERIALS

metal lunch pail

22" (56cm) of ⅜" (10mm) two-tone
polka dot ribbon

⅞" (22mm) wide satin ribbon

yellow silk daisy flowers

clear alphabet dimensional stickers

white paper

¼" (6mm) wide double-sided craft tape

clear nail polish

tip > To add color to clear dome stickers, place them on a sheet of colored paper. For this project, I used white paper to contrast with the yellow petals.

ANOTHER SIMPLY BEAUTIFUL IDEA

For the holidays, switch the ribbon colors to red and green. Line the inside of the tin with wax paper and pack it with a selection of homemade fudge, candies and cookies.

This personalized tin isn't just for lunch! It makes a great gift box for both children and the young at heart. For a back-to-school surprise, fill the finished tin with school supplies, or for a birthday gift fill it with hair accessories and cosmetics. This carryall will surely have a long shelf life beautifully organizing odds and ends.

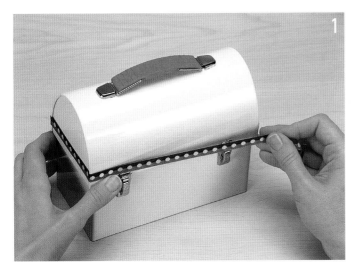

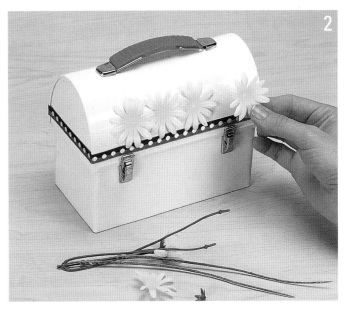

one • Apply double-sided craft tape around the lunch pail lid. Position the bottom edge of the tape above the top of the metal hinges. Peel off the backing to expose the adhesive. Starting at the back of the pail, press the polka dot ribbon into the adhesive. When you've encircled the entire lid with ribbon, trim away any excess length and apply clear nail polish to the cut ends to prevent fraying.

two • Cut off the flower stems and pull out the flower centers so that you are left with only the silk flower petals. Repeat the process until you have a flower petal for each letter in the desired name. Use small pieces of double-sided craft tape to attach the back of each petal onto the pail. Center the petals in a straight line above the ribbon.

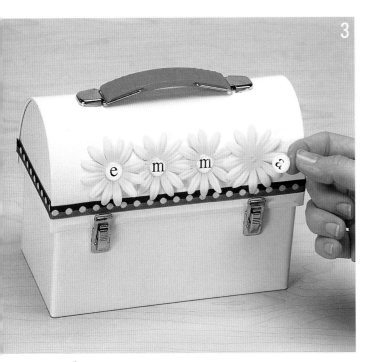

four • Tie the satin ribbon in a bow around one side of the handle.

three • Apply the dimensional alphabet stickers onto a sheet of white paper. Cut the stickers off the page and use small pieces of double-sided craft tape to attach them to the centers of the silk petals.

*tip > The finished pail is not waterproof! If necessary, wipe clean with a damp cloth. Do not submerge in water.

travel case

MATERIALS

pink quilted place mat

two 6¾" (17cm) x 11½" (29cm) rectangles
of heavyweight clear vinyl
(sold by the yard in fabric stores)

2" (5cm) wide toile ribbon

9⁄16" (14mm) wide gingham ribbon

⅛" (3mm) wide black satin ribbon

¼" (6mm) wide black satin ribbon

pearl button

black elastic beading cord

textile glue

fusible tape

clear nail polish

sewing machine and pink thread
(or match thread to placemat color)

sewing needle

iron

P retty in pink! This surprising travel bag is made out of a
quilted place mat. Unfold the envelope to find two over-
sized clear pockets that keep toiletries within view. The
romantic toile ribbon, little black bows and pearl button make
this feminine bag a perfect wedding shower gift. Fill it with
travel-sized cosmetics so the bride can simply pack it into her
honeymoon luggage.

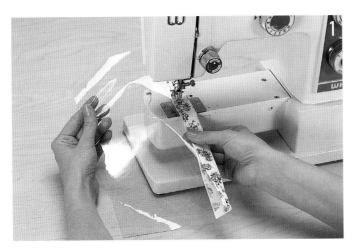

one · Fold the toile ribbon in half over the top of one of the vinyl rectangles. Machine stitch a seam ¼" (6mm) from the ribbon edge, trapping the top edge of the vinyl between the folded ribbon. Repeat the process to edge the top of the second vinyl rectangle with toile ribbon.

two · Machine stitch the sides and bottom edges of the vinyl directly onto the place mat. Position the bottom pocket 1" (3cm) from the left side of the place mat, and the top pocket 5" (13cm) from the right side of the place mat. Center the pockets

1¾" (4cm) from the top and bottom edges of the place mat. Place a length of gingham ribbon over the bare vinyl edges before you stitch the pockets in place. This will keep the sewing machine from stitching directly over the vinyl.

three · To decorate the front flap, flip the place mat over and apply several lengths of fusible tape 1" (3cm) from the right edge. Remove the paper backing and lay a length of gingham and toile ribbon over the exposed adhesive. Iron the ribbons in place to activate the fusible tape.

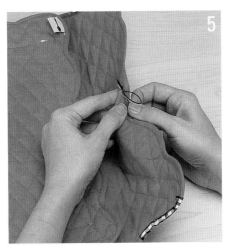

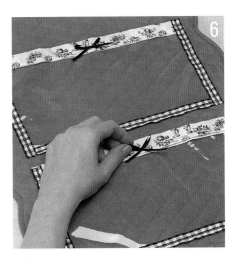

four · To finish the ends of the fused ribbon, cut two 2½" (6cm) lengths of gingham ribbon and seal their edges with nail polish. Apply textile glue to the underside of one of the prepared ribbons and press it over one side of the place mat, covering both the toile and gingham ribbons ends. Apply more glue to the other ribbon and press it over the other side of the place mat to cover the other end of the ribbons.

five · Fold a short length of black elastic in half and tie it in an overhand knot. Stitch the knot to the underside of the front flap so the loop extends out from the center. Fold up the bottom pocket so the travel bag takes its finished shape. Place the button on the underside of the bottom pocket and check its position with the elastic loop before sewing it in place.

six · Tie two bows out of ⅛" (3mm) wide black ribbon. Use textile glue to attach one bow to the center of the toile ribbon on each pocket. Make a third bow out of the ¼" (6mm) wide black ribbon. Use more textile glue to attach this bow to the center of the fused ribbon on the front flap. Let the glued bows dry completely before using the finished travel bag.

drawstring sachet

MATERIALS

5" x 6½" (13cm x 17cm) sheer pouch

dried lavender or rose petals

11" (28cm) of ⅜" (10mm) wide
ivory feather-edged ribbon

11" (28cm) of ¼" (6mm) wide
gold feather-edged ribbon

¼" (6mm) wide iridescent ribbon

1½" (4cm) wide sequined
and beaded ribbon

4⅜" x 5¼" (11cm x 13cm)
piece of cardboard

½" (13mm) wide fusible tape

clear nail polish

iron

clean, plain cloth

Too beautiful to hide away in your dresser drawer, this one-of-a-kind sachet will most likely stay out on display. A simple drawstring bag is the perfect backdrop for your collection of ribbon scraps. Juxtapose different colors, widths and varieties together to make a unique sachet.

ANOTHER SIMPLY BEAUTIFUL IDEA

Smaller in stature but still captivating, this little bag has sparkle. Simply add a strip of fusible tape to the bottom of the sachet to add a fringe of beaded trim. These sachets make beautiful gifts or wedding shower favors. Fill them with herbs that impart special significance. For instance, marjoram signifies remembrance.

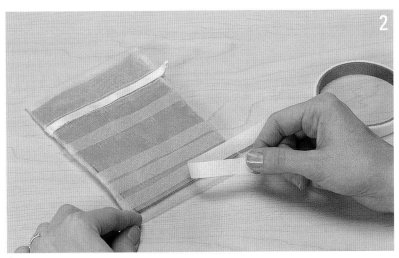

one · Place cardboard inside the sheer pouch, it will prevent the adhesive from seeping through the sheer fabric.

two · Wrap fusible tape from front to back around the sachet. Position a piece of tape for each length of ribbon you're planning on using.

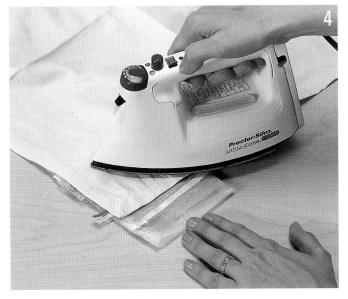

three · Peel off the paper backing from the fusible tape and wrap a ribbon length over each adhesive strip. If you're using narrow ribbon, place ribbons side by side so the adhesive is completely covered.

four · Place a press cloth over the front of the sachet, then iron the sachet. The heat will activate the fusible tape and anchor the ribbon to the sachet. Turn the sachet over and make any necessary positioning adjustments before replacing the press cloth and ironing the other side of the sachet.

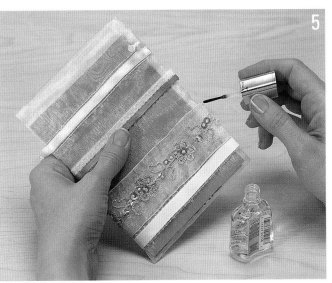

five · Trim the ribbon ends and apply clear nail polish to the cut ends to prevent them from fraying. Remove the cardboard and fill the sachet with dried lavender or rose petals.

bookmark

MATERIALS

11" (28cm) of ⅞" (22mm) wide
Jacquard ribbon

11" (28cm) of 1¼" (3cm) wide
black satin ribbon

11" (28cm) of 1½" (4cm) wide
gray/silver wire-edged ribbon

scrapbook embellishment
(silver rim alphabet)

8mm jump ring

½" (13mm) wide fusible tape

clear nail polish

eyelet

craft hammer and eyelet setter

round-nose pliers

⅛" (3mm) hole punch

pressing cloth

iron

tip > Don't worry if you can't find the identical initial tag. You can easily substitute cut metal letters, charms or even drop crystal beads. Just be sure your selection has a ready-made hole at the top so that it'll hang freely from the jump ring.

Mark your page with this stylish personalized bookmark. The solid black and gray ribbon makes the perfect backdrop to showcase ornate jacquard ribbon. Use your paper crafting skills to set a rivet into the ribbon to hang an initial tag.

one • Apply fusible tape down the center of the gray ribbon. Remove the paper backing and lay the black ribbon over the exposed tape. Iron the stacked ribbon to activate the fusible tape.

two • Apply a second strip of tape down the center of the black ribbon and apply the jacquard ribbon over the tape. Iron it in place.

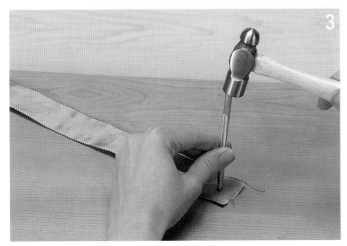

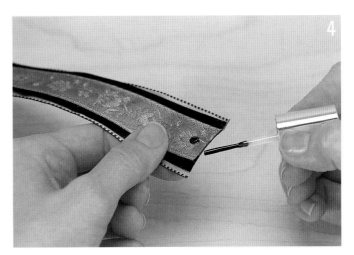

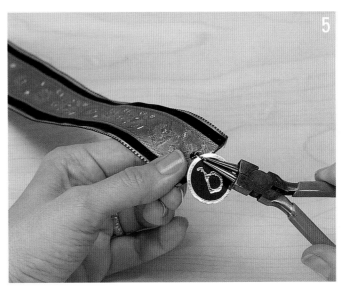

three • At the base of the fused ribbons, punch a ⅛" (3mm) hole through all the layers of fused ribbons. Use the eyelet setter and craft hammer to set an eyelet in the hole.

four • Trim straight across the top and bottom of the ribbon to even the ends. Apply nail polish to all three layers to prevent fraying.

five • Use round-nose pliers to laterally open the jump ring. Hook the jump ring through the set eyelet. Thread the initial tag onto the base of the open ring, then use pliers to close the ring.

journal

MATERIALS

5½" x 8" (14cm x 20cm) blank journal

16½" (42cm) of 1½" (4cm) wide
flowered satin ribbon

¼" (6mm) wide red grosgrain ribbon

silk flower

½" (13mm) wide double-sided craft tape

¾" x ¾" (19mm x 19mm) wide Velcro

fabric adhesive

masking tape

mechanical pencil

This plain leather journal is the perfect backdrop for richly patterned poppy ribbon. The decorative ribbon is functional as well. Velcro is applied to the ribbon ends to keep the journal securely closed while in transit. To complete the gift set, make the matching mechanical pencil too. Unlike the flower-topped pens you find by cash registers, the flower can be removed so new lead can be easily inserted.

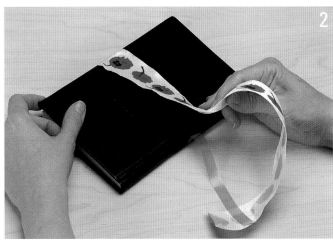

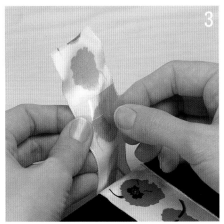

one · Use a small piece of double-sided craft tape to fold under ¼" (6mm) of the flowered satin ribbon end. Place the end of the double-sided craft tape just inside the front cover, and then wrap the length of the tape across the front cover, spine and back cover. Peel the tape backing off the small section of tape inside the front cover and stick the prepared ribbon end to the adhesive.

two · Peel off the next section of tape backing to expose the adhesive on the front cover and spine.

Tightly wrap the ribbon around the front of the book, pressing the fabric into the tape. Peel off the remaining backing and finish wrapping the ribbon across the back of the journal.

three · Working on the underside of the ribbon, apply a small piece of tape 1" (3cm) below the ribbon end, then fold the end down into the tape. This finished end will form a small strap that will partially overlap the front of the journal to secure it closed.

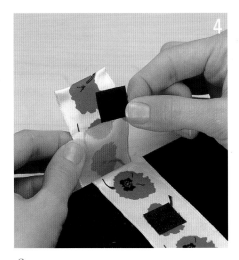

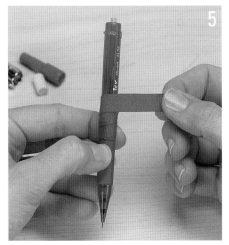

four · Use double-sided craft tape to attach the Velcro (stiff part) to the ribbon on the front of the journal, and another piece of Velcro (fuzzy) to the underside of the strap. Make sure the Velcro pieces are properly aligned before taping them in place.

five · Pull the top and metal pocket clip off the pencil and discard the eraser, but retain the plastic holder and clip. Apply two strips of double-sided craft tape up either side of the pencil, stopping ¼" (6mm) from the top. Peel off the backing and tightly wrap grosgrain ribbon up the pencil, starting just above the tip end and ending where the tape stops. Use fabric adhesive to adhere the ribbon end flush against the wrapped ribbon.

six · Slide the metal pocket clip and plastic pencil top back in place. Cut the silk poppy off the stem and remove the plastic leaf ring under the petals. Squeeze a generous amount of adhesive into the opened plastic pencil top. Insert the flower stem end first into the adhesive. Use a long piece of masking tape to hold the flower down while the adhesive dries. Stand the pencil flower end up in a glass to keep the drying adhesive from dripping.

ribbon sketchbook

MATERIALS

6" x 8" (15cm x 20cm) sketchbook

28" (71cm) length of 2½" (6cm) wide
brocade ribbon

9" x 13" (23cm x 33cm) wide
pig suede leather
(I used Leather Factory brand)

two 18½" (47cm) lengths of leather lace

sewing machine and green thread

straight pins

For creative types on the go, this case keeps pencil and paper close at hand. When inspiration hits, set the book on your knee and start sketching. The ornate bee ribbon is not only decorative, it's both sturdy and wide enough to make secure pockets for the pencils, pens and sketchbook.

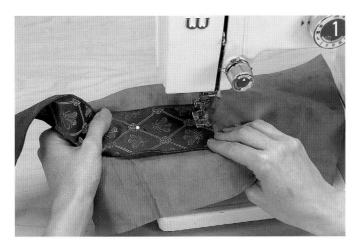

one · Begin working on the inside (suede side) of the leather sketch-book cover. Fold the leather in half to locate the center. Drape the ribbon over the left side of the leather and position the ribbon end against the center. Attach the ribbon end to the leather with a vertical line of stitching.

two · Make eight more vertical seams down the ribbon. Space each seam ¾" (19mm) apart to make seven pencil pockets. Trim the threads.

three · Turn the leather over to work on the outside of the cover. Bring the ribbon around the leather edge and lay its length across the center of the outside (smooth side) of the cover. Slip the center of a leather lace under the ribbon so it rests against the left leather edge. Make a vertical line of stitching right alongside the leather edge to hold the lace in place.

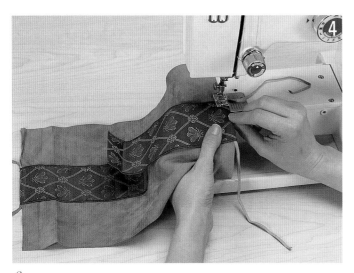

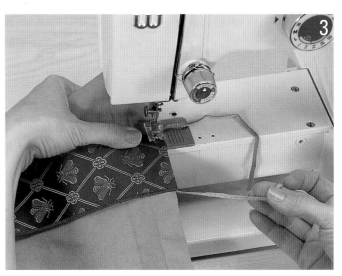

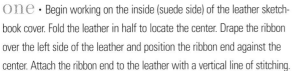

four · Turn the leather over to work on the inside again. Bring the ribbon end around the right leather edge so the remaining length rests across the right side of the cover. Slip the center of the second lace under the ribbon and make a vertical line of stitching against the right leather edge to hold it in place.

five · Tuck under ¼" (6mm) of the ribbon end and make a final vertical line of stitching to attach the ribbon end to the center of the cover. This seam serves two purposes: It anchors the middle of the ribbon that spans across the outside of the cover and it creates a sleeve inside the cover for the sketchbook to slide into.

jewelry & accessories

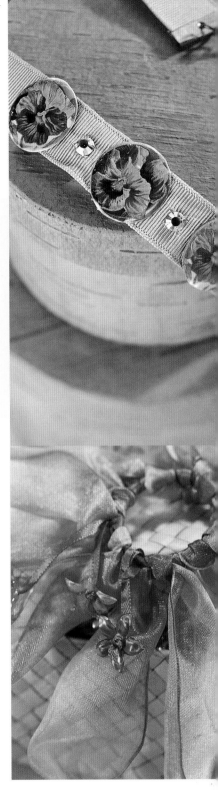

r ibbons and beads are the perfect marriage of materials when they readily combine to make beautiful necklaces. With the help of a few jewelry findings, glue, and sewing needles you'll have all you need to transform ribbon into stunning accessories to complement your wardrobe.

Attractive all on its own, thin silk ribbon effortlessly strings through silver beads to make the multi-strand choker. Delicate organdy ribbon creates a graceful featherweight choker that is even more interesting when punctuated by wired glass flowers and leaf beads. Made almost exclusively out of ribbon, the pendant purse begins with a folded section of brocade ribbon. It sparkles with stitched swinging beaded trim, crystal and seed beads. Antique floral motifs and dazzling rhinestones are glued and riveted to heavy grosgrain ribbon to make nostalgic costume jewelry pieces.

Spiraled into roses or wrapped and tied in bows, ribbons quickly become beautiful hair accessories. For a tailored fashion statement make the chic ribbon barrettes, but if your tastes run romantic ruffle up rose pins, barrettes or ponytail holders. For little girls who love to dress up like a princess, save money by making pink and purple beaded ponytail holders from ribbon scraps. For more formal occasions, make a ruffled rose headband that coordinates with party frocks for a special occasion.

There are so many ways to spice up your wardrobe with ribbons. Trim a handbag with a fluttering ribbon ruffle or wrap ribbon around a wooden box to make a unique cigar box purse. All the projects are quick to make, but you'll find yourself enjoying their longevity when you wear them over and over again.

CHAPTER

4

ribbon barrettes

MATERIALS

3" (8cm) metal barrette

1⅛" x 3¾" (3cm x 10cm) piece of cardboard

8½" (22cm) of 1¼" (3cm) wide black feather-edged ribbon

18" (46cm) of ⅜" (10mm) wide white wire-edged ribbon

Aleene's Textile glue

clothespins

T hese classically tailored barrettes will add style to any outfit. The black and white ribbons both contrast and complement each other to make chic hair accessories. Experiment by pairing different ribbon colors and varieties together to make unique barrettes that coordinate with your wardrobe.

ANOTHER SIMPLY BEAUTIFUL IDEA

Playful polka dots add to the charm of this child-sized barrette. It's ideally sized to hold little locks in place. Wrap a ¼" x 2¼" (6mm x 6cm) long piece of cardboard with a 5½" (14cm) long piece of ⅜" (10mm) wide white wired ribbon. Tie a ⅛" (3mm) wide polka dot ribbon around the white ribbon. Glue a 1½" (4cm) barrette back under the wrapped and tied barrette.

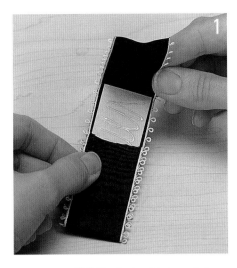

two • Add more glue over the middle of the ribbon ends. Position the center of the 18" (46cm) piece of white wired ribbon over the glue. Bring the ends of the white ribbon around the sides to the front of the barrette and then tie the ends into a bow.

three • Apply glue along the back of the cardboard and then press the metal barrette back into the glue. While the glue dries, clamp the cardboard to the metal with clothespins.

one • Apply a thin layer of glue to both sides of the cardboard. Center the cardboard in the middle of the 8½" (22cm) length of feather-edged ribbon. Fold the ribbon ends up over the cardboard sides and press them into the glue to secure.

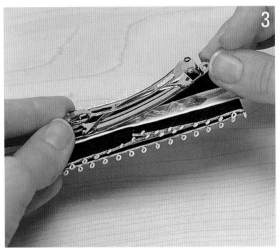

gingham barrette

houndstooth barrette

ANOTHER SIMPLY BEAUTIFUL IDEA

Custom tailor the size of the barrettes for how you style your hair, and the variety of ribbons offers an almost limitless number of barrette possibilities. The gingham barrette is perfectly sized to pull strands of hair back off the sides of your face. Start with a 1½" (4cm) x 2¼" (6cm) piece of cardboard and cover it with a ⅝" (16mm) wide and 5" (13cm) long gingham ribbon. Tie a ⅛" (3mm) wide black ribbon in a bow around the center of the gingham ribbon. Glue a 1½" (4cm) long metal barrette back under the wrapped and tied barrette. The bold houndstooth barrette is large enough to pull all your hair back into a ponytail or hold it in a twist against the back of your head. It is made exactly like the feathered edged barrette, but is tied with ⅜" (10mm) wide black ribbon instead of white ribbon.

ribbon rose pin

MATERIALS

1" (3cm) pin back

22" (56cm) of 1" (3cm) wide
wire-edged ribbon

fire polished crystal beads

two 4" (10cm) pieces of thin floral wire

wired floral leaf

sewing needle and thread

round-nose pliers

tip > Before ruffling the ribbon, apply nail polish to the cut ribbon edges. This will prolong the life of the silk flower.

Ruffle ribbon into beautifully blooming flowers. Paired with silk leaves and crystal bead centers, these colorful flowers sparkle. Simply pinch the ribbon with your fingertips to reposition the petals and keep them from wilting. Use this versatile pin to add an unexpected splash of color to a dress, lapel, hat brim or purse. The easy-to-use pin back makes switching the pin's placement a snap.

one · Hold the two lengths of thin floral wire together and fold them in half. Working on the underside of the pinback, thread a pair of wire ends up through each hole in the pin back. Thread a bead onto each separate wire end. Use round-nose pliers to bend over the wire ends so the beads are anchored in place.

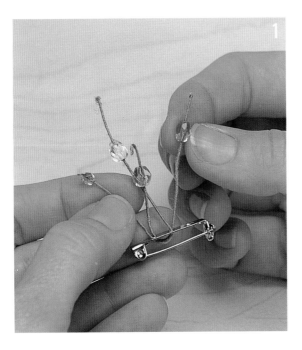

two · Thread the leaf stem down through one hole and then bring it back up through the second hole. Spiral the end of the leaf stem around the round-nose pliers.

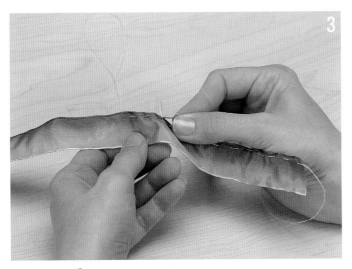

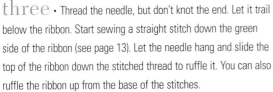

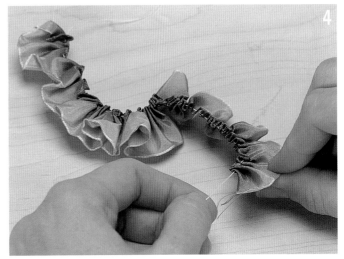

three · Thread the needle, but don't knot the end. Let it trail below the ribbon. Start sewing a straight stitch down the green side of the ribbon (see page 13). Let the needle hang and slide the top of the ribbon down the stitched thread to ruffle it. You can also ruffle the ribbon up from the base of the stitches.

four · The flower is wrapped and tied around the wired bead centers. Turn the pin over and pull, then knot the thread ends together.

five · Cut off the needle and begin spiraling the gathered ribbon into a flower shape around the wired bead flower center. The flower should sit over the leaf.

RIBBON ROSE BARRETTE

● **RIBBON FLOWERS MAKE FABULOUS** hair accessories. For instant elegance, simply clip this barrette into curled or twisted hair. Be sure to select a barrette back that fits the thickness of your hair. The flower and leaves can be fastened to any size clip.

MATERIALS

metal barrette

1½" (4cm) wide wired ribbon

fire-polished crystal beads

two 4" (10cm) pieces of thin floral wire

round-nose pliers

sewing needle and thread

one • Hold the floral wires together and fold them in half. Hook the folded wire around the center of the barrette back and twist the wires together. Add beads to the end of each wire and fold the wire ends over. Thread the leaf stem through one hole and then up through another hole. Hot glue the underside of the leaf over one end of the barrette. Spiral the stem wires around round-nose pliers. Position the shaped wire over the other end of a barrette.

two • Use a ruffle stitch on the dark blue side of the ribbon to make a flower. Wrap the flower around the beaded flower center. Pull and knot the threads under the barrette back to secure the ribbon to the barrette.

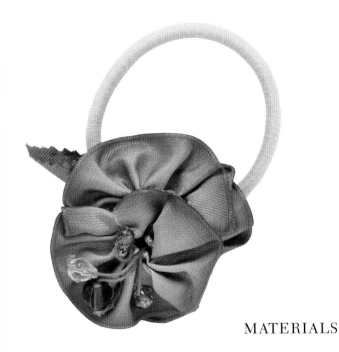

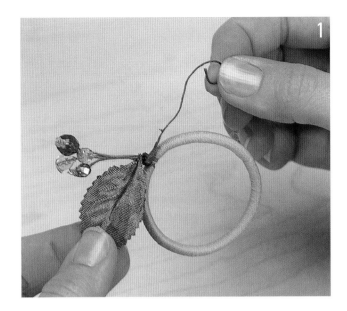

MATERIALS

elastic band

⅞" (22mm) wide wired ribbon

single leaf

fire-polished crystal beads

two 4" (10cm) lengths of floral wire

sewing needle and thread

ROSE PONYTAIL HOLDER

• ADD GLAMOUR TO YOUR EVERYDAY

style. Next time you pull your hair up into

a ponytail, loop a silk flower ponytail holder

into place. It's so comfortable, you won't

even remember it's there.

one • Loop the center of the floral wires around the ponytail holder and twist the wires together to anchor them in place. Thread a bead onto each wire end and fold the wire ends over to hold them in place. Twist the leaf stem around the base of the floral wires. Trim away any excess stem.

two • Ruffle stitch down the green side of the ribbon to make a purple flower. Wrap the flower around the beaded flower center. Pull and knot the thread ends together under the flower.

tip > Increase the length and width of the ribbon to make a fuller ribbon

rose. Decrease the length and width of the ribbon to make a smaller rose. You

can also alter the rose's appearance by drawing more attention to the flower cen-

ter with larger crystal beads or less attention with smaller beads.

ponytail holder

For head to toe glamour, these shimmering ponytail holders will add pizzazz to everyday wear. Perfect for girls who love to play dress up, the wired ribbons won't lose their shape, and the beaded flowers will flounce with every step.

ANOTHER SIMPLY BEAUTIFUL IDEA

Purple and pink are popular colors with young ladies. Simply switch the hair band and bead colors to match the desired ribbon color. Look for a selection of all these organdy ribbon colors in spring ribbon displays.

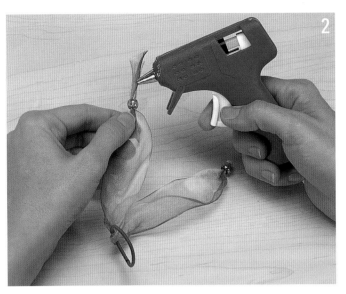

one · Tie the center of an organdy ribbon around the elastic hair band.

two · Thread a single bead onto each ribbon end. Working with one end at a time, slide the bead down and add a dot of hot glue just below the ribbon end. Slide the bead back up over the glue to anchor it to the ribbon end. Trim the ends above the bead and apply nail polish to the cut ends. Repeat steps 1 and 2 six more times to make a total of fourteen beaded organdy ribbon ends hanging from the hair band.

three · Loop the folded center of a 7" (18cm) satin ribbon up through the middle of the hair band. Thread the satin ribbon ends up through the loop, securing them to the hair band.

four · Thread a plastic flower bead to each ribbon end. Make one or two overhand knots at each ribbon end to prevent the bead from sliding off. Repeat steps 3 and 4 six times to attach a total of seven satin ribbons between the organdy ribbons.

gingham headband

fabric covered headband

24" (61cm) of 1½" (4cm) wide
wire-edged ribbon

14¾" (37cm) ribbon roses

glue gun

clear nail polish

sewing needle and thread

ANOTHER SIMPLY BEAUTIFUL IDEA

To make a headband for a flower girl, start with a white or ivory headband and satin ribbon. Select ornate beaded or sequined ribbon roses to top the ruffled ribbon.

This playful hair accessory with classic styling is perfect for both casual and formal occasions. The headband is deceivingly quick and simple to make, and can be easily customized to match a special holiday dress.

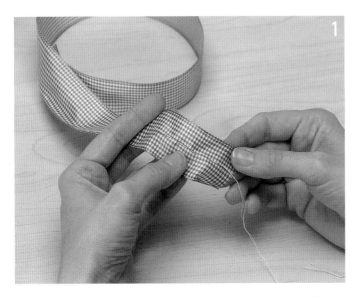

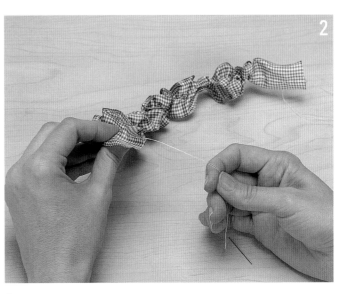

one · Thread the needle, but don't knot the end. Begin stitching up the middle of the wire-edged ribbon. Allow a couple inches of thread to hang below the ribbon end.

two · Create ruffles by gently sliding the ribbon down the thread until it bunches. You can also ruffle the ribbon up from the base by sliding the ribbon up the thread. Wrap the ruffled ribbon around the headband and adjust it so that the ribbon ends are smooth and the ruffles crown the top.

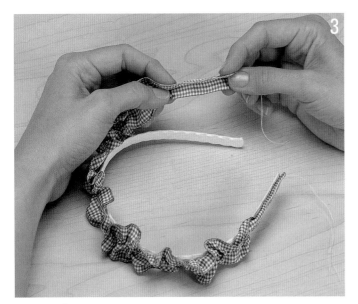

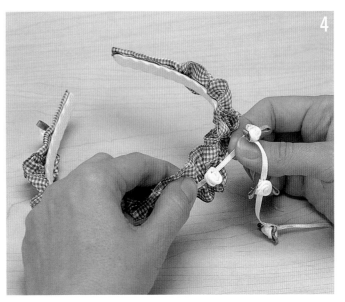

three · To narrow the ribbon end, fold and glue the sides of the ribbon under the center of the ribbon. Hot glue the folded ribbon end to one end of the headband. Continue gluing the ruffled ribbon over the top of the headband. Finish by narrowing the other ribbon end and gluing it to the other end of the headband. Cut the sewing needle from the threads.

four · Starting on one side of the headband, hot glue the flower trim over the center of the ruffled ribbon. Cover the stitches as you glue the flower trim. Trim the ribbon and thread ends flush with the ends of the headband and apply nail polish to the cut ends to prevent fraying.

antique choker

MATERIALS

dimensional stickers

copper colored metal sheet (ArtEmboss)

15" (38cm) of ⅝" (16mm) wide grosgrain ribbon

flower stickers

two rhinestones with pronged metal setting bases

jewelry glue (I used Aleene's Platinum Bond Glass and Bead glue)

small screwdriver

hook and eye clasp

1/16" (2mm) hole punch

round-nose pliers

S turdy grosgrain ribbon serves as a resilient base for this costume jewelry. Simulating glass, the clear domed plastic stickers distort flower stickers, making them intriguing focal points. Metal scraps embellish the images and finish the ribbon edges, and rhinestones add sparkle to the ribbon.

ANOTHER SIMPLY BEAUTIFUL IDEA

Use 6½" (17cm) of ⅝" (16mm) wide length of grosgrain ribbon to make the bracelet. The center of the bracelet is a mounted rose sticker under one side of a dimensional sticker. Use letter stickers over the other side of the domed sticker. Follow steps 4 and 5 to finish the ribbon edges and apply the clasp. Remove the bracelet before washing hands or doing housework to keep it clean and dry.

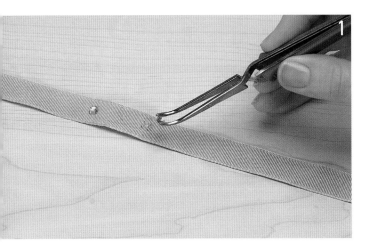

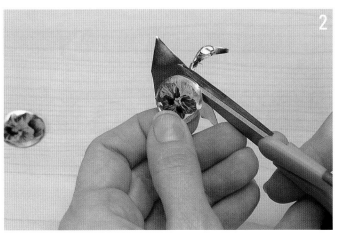

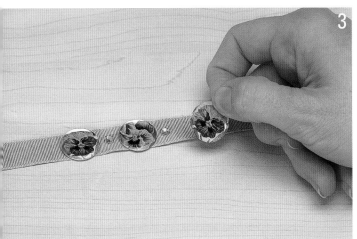

 one · Fold the ribbon in half to locate the center. Position a rhinestone base 1" (3cm) from either side of the center point. Push each metal base, with the prong side up, through the underside of the ribbon. Insert a rhinestone into each base and use a flat screwdriver tip to press the prongs flat against the rhinestones to anchor them in place.

two · Place flower stickers on a metal scrap. Apply a dimensional sticker over each mounted flower sticker. Trim around the domed sticker to remove the excess metal. Repeat this step to create two more flower motifs.

three · Use jewelry glue to attach the metal backed motifs onto the grosgrain ribbon. Center one between the rhinestones and position the other two on either side. Don't disturb the flowers until the glue sets.

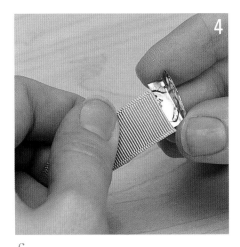

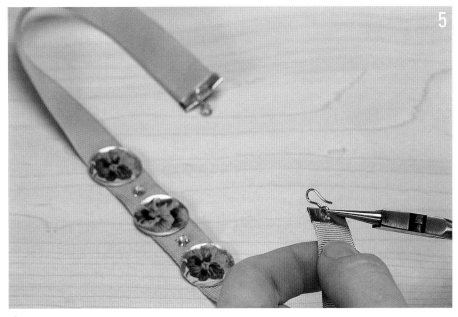

four · Pinch a ½" x ⅝" (13mm x 16mm) metal piece lengthwise. Add a small amount of jewelry glue inside the folded metal. Slide the metal, glue side first, over a ribbon end, then squeeze it flat. The metal should completely encase the ribbon end. Repeat to cover the other ribbon end.

five · With a 1⁄16" (2mm) hole punch, punch a hole through the center of each metal end. Use round-nose pliers to thread one part of the hook and eye clasp through each punched hole.

multi-strand choker

20" (51cm) strands of ivory, tan and light green 4mm silk embroidery ribbon

silver beads: bicone, round

cat's eyes: round and cube in ivory, light green and tan

spring clasp

end cups (to cover the knot)

sewing needle

needle-nose pliers

tip > Look for packets of specialty ribbon intended for embroidery in fabric or craft stores. It's made of hundred percent silk fibers and is available in a range of subtle colors. Ideal for jewelry making, the ribbon threads easily through the eye of a small needle.

M atching shades of silk ribbon, cat's eye beads and silver accents quickly come together to make this a beautiful, understated necklace. The featherlight ribbon will caress your neck and the simple design will add elegance to any outfit.

one · Tie three silk embroidery ribbon ends together in an overhand knot. Pull the knot tight.

two · Trap the knot inside the end cup and squeeze the cup closed with needle-nose pliers. Trim away any ribbon ends that extend beyond the end cup.

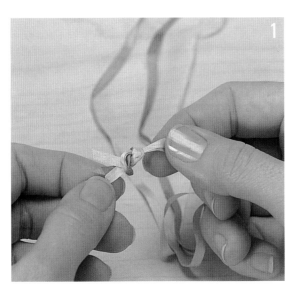

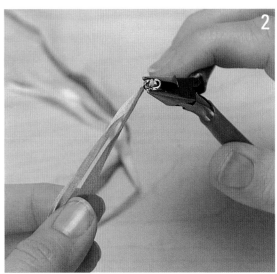

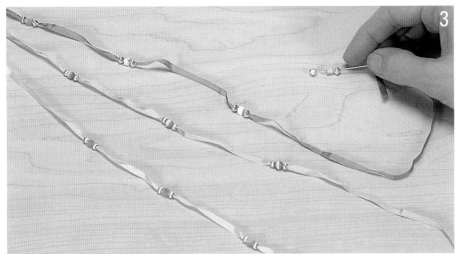

three · Thread a needle onto one of the ribbon ends. Use the needle to string a bead sequence (silver, cat's eye and then silver) on the ribbon. Add three to four bead sequences on the ribbon length, spacing each of the bead groupings 2" (5cm) apart. Remove the needle and repeat the process with the two remaining ribbon lengths. Use tan cat's eyes on the ivory strand, ivory beads on the tan strand and green beads on the green strand.

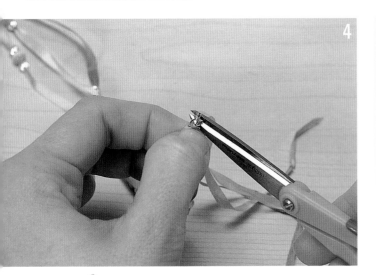

four · Tie the end of all three ribbons in an overhand knot; the positioning of this knot will determine the finished length of your necklace. Trap the knot inside an end cup, and squeeze the cup closed with needle-nose pliers. If necessary, trim away stray ribbon ends.

five · Hook one half of the clasp through the loop in the top of the end cup. Use needle-nose pliers to bend the loop closed and trap the clasp in place. Repeat the process to attach the other half of the clasp to the other end cup.

organdy choker

MATERIALS

2' (1m) of ½" (13mm) wide
organdy ribbon

leaf beads

flower beads

turquoise and yellow seed beads

32-gauge gold beading wire

barrel clasp

ANOTHER SIMPLY BEAUTIFUL IDEA

This choker, made with ivory ribbon and white and ivory beads, would make a fabulous bridal accessory.

This delicate choker is made with featherlight organdy ribbon. The ribbon is knotted at intervals and then accented with tiny seed beads and glass flower and leaf beads. The finished choker has an almost ethereal quality as the translucent beads and ribbon reflect and diffuse light.

one · Loop one end of the ribbon through one half of the barrel clasp.

two · Tie the ribbon in an overhand knot, trapping the clasp in a 1½" (4cm) loop. The ribbon end should be trapped in the knot. If necessary, trim it flush with the knot.

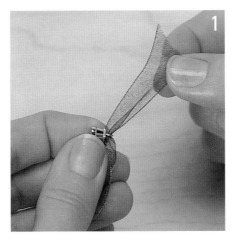

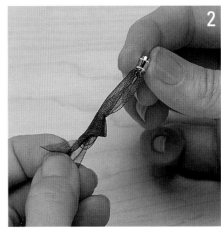

three · Twist a leaf bead onto the end of a short length of beading wire, then string five turquoise seed beads to make a stem. Wrap the wired leaf and stem around the ribbon just before the knot. Twist the wire end back around the base of the leaf bead and then trim the wire.

four · Pass a second length of wire up through a flower bead and a yellow seed bead flower center. Bring the wire back down through the flower and twist the wire back around itself at the flower base. String five turquoise seed beads to make a stem. Wrap the wired stem and flower around the ribbon just after the knot. Twist the wire end around the base of the flower bead and trim the wire.

five · Make a second overhand knot with a single thickness of ribbon 2" (5cm) from the first knot. Repeat steps 3 and 4 to decorate the knot with beads. Make three more beaded knots spaced 2" (5cm) apart. Finish by adding the other end of the clasp. The knots should be 2" (5cm) apart, and there should be 1½" (4cm) between the first and last knots and the clasps. Thread the end of the ribbon through the other half of the barrel clasp and anchor it in place with an overhand knot that traps the ribbon end. Trim the ribbon end and decorate the knot with wired beads.

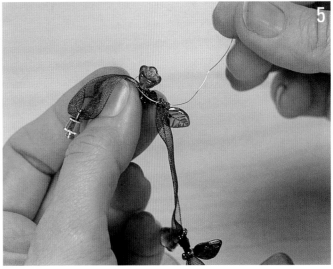

pendant purse

36" (91cm) of ⅛" (3mm) wide satin ribbon

4" (10cm) of 1⅜" (3cm) wide jacquard ribbon

beaded trim

eight brown seed beads

three crystal beads (two bicones)

textile or fabric glue

sewing needle and thread

This clever little purse is a cinch to make and is almost completely assembled with different varieties of ribbon. Jacquard ribbon folds in half to make the purse. Beaded ribbon trim decorates the bottom edge and narrow satin ribbon makes the elongated strap.

ANOTHER SIMPLY BEAUTIFUL IDEA

The possible combinations of jacquard ribbons and beaded ribbon trims are endless. Experiment with different colors and patterns. You're assured success if you color coordinate the narrow ribbon strap and accent beads with your selections.

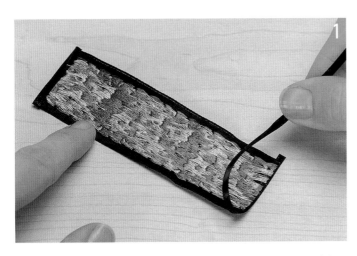

one · Glue a length of ⅛" (3mm) wide black satin around the front and back of the cut edges at the top and bottom of the jacquard ribbon. This will give the jacquard ribbon a finished edge and prevent it from fraying.

two · Thread the needle with black thread and stitch three crystal beads to the center top of the jacquard ribbon. Knot and trim the thread ends on the underside of the ribbon.

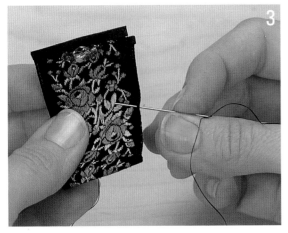

three · Fold the jacquard ribbon in half and sew up one side of the folded ribbon. Stop just below the black satin ribbon edge.

four · Trap one end of the 36" (91cm) long ⅛" (3mm) wide satin ribbon strap in your next stitch. Make a second decorative stitch over the first connection, this time threading four seed beads onto the needle before completing the stitch. Repeat steps 3 and 4 to sew up the other side of the purse and connect the other side of the ribbon strap. To help shape the strap, tie the center of the ribbon into a loose overhand knot.

five · Glue the beaded trim around the front and back of the bottom of the purse. Make sure the ends of the ribbon are tucked under and trapped in the glue so they don't unravel.

ribbon handbag

MATERIALS

standard cotton place mat

5½" x 3¾" (14cm x 10cm) silver handle frame

assorted ribbon: ⅞" to 2" wide (22mm to 5cm) and 7" to 8½" (18cm x 22cm) in length

pony beads (or other beads whose openings are wide enough to accommodate the wire handle)

sewing machine and thread

sewing needle and thread

tip > If you don't like the intentional frayed look of the ribbon ruffle, apply nail polish to the cut ribbon ends before stitching them onto the handbag. This will prevent the ribbon from fraying.

Fluttering along the top edge of this little handbag are eye-catching ribbons. This sturdy little bag is simply made with a folded place mat. What makes it appealing is the interesting mix of ribbons that surround the top edge. The wire handles are strung with beads that complement the colors in the ribbons.

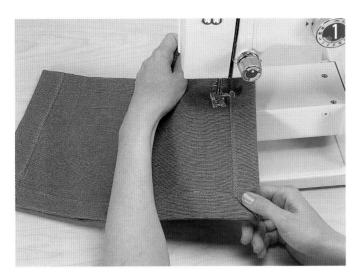

one · Fold the place mat in half, bringing the sides together. Machine stitch a diagonal seam up either side of the folded place mat. Start stitching along the bottom folded edge 2¾" (7cm) from the outside corners, and end each seam ½" (13mm) from the outside corners of the open top edge.

two · Turn the bag right side out and position the top edge under the presser foot. Begin sliding the center of the ribbons right side down under the needle so that they cover the top edge of the purse. Overlap the ribbons and mix the different colors and varieties of ribbons together. Make a single seam around the top of the purse to hold the ribbons in place. Stop sewing occasionally to slide more ribbons into position before continuing the seam.

three · Fold the top half of the ribbons down (so they're right side up) and stitch a second seam around the top of the bag, position this seam just under the first one. You'll need to stop every few inches to fold the tops of the next few ribbons down before continuing the seam.

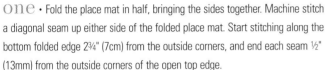

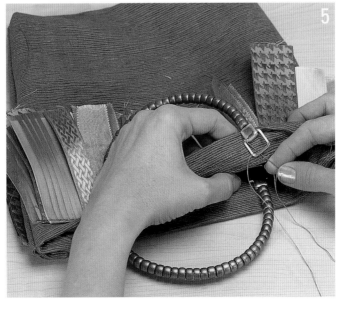

four · Unscrew one of the bases from the wire handle and thread pony beads onto the wire. Once the handle is completely filled with beads, replace the base. Repeat the process to bead the second handle.

five · Use a sewing needle and thread to hand stitch the handle bases to the inside top of the purse. Make multiple stitches and tie the thread ends in tight knots so that the handles are firmly secured to the bag.

cigar box purse

MATERIALS

Mod Podge decoupage medium

6½" x 10" x 2" (17cm x 25cm x 5cm)
wooden cigar box [Out of the Box Purses]

natural bamboo handle
[Out of the Box Purses]

lock: vintage clasp with screws
[Out of the Box Purses]

metal scrapbooking frame [Metal Art]

two 18" (46cm) lengths of 3" (8cm) wide
beige and dark brown wired ribbon

1 yard (1m) of 1½" (4cm) wide
black and tan wire-edged ribbon

4 sheets of patterned scrapbook paper

stickers [P. Real Life]

double-sided craft tape

clear nail polish

paintbrush

small screwdriver

NOTE: Different size purses may
require different ribbon lengths

tip > Handles, hardware and hinged wooden boxes are readily available in craft stores.

Wide striped ribbon and scrapbook paper quickly transform a plain wooden box into a stylish purse. Fully functional, the purse has sturdy handles and a clasp that easily opens and closes. A clear coat of découpage medium protects the interior and exterior of the purse.

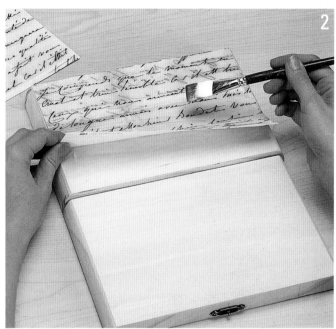

one · Use a small screwdriver to screw the clasp to the center top of the wooden box. It will be much easier to drive the ornate screws into the wood if you mark the clasp placement with a pencil and pre-drill the holes with a small drill bit.

two · Open the box and lay it, outside up, on your work surface. Start at the top and brush découpage medium over one side of the box. Mount the scrapbook paper over the glue, aligning the top edge and corners of the paper with the top edge and corners of the box. Working top to bottom, brush more medium over and under the paper to smooth out any air bubbles until the entire length of scrapbook paper is mounted to the box. Repeat the process to mount the second sheet of paper to the other side of the box. Allow the glue to dry completely before continuing.

three · Close the box and wrap double-sided craft tape around the center of each of the two sides of the box. Inside the box apply four more small strips of tape against the box sides. Avoid placing tape on the rim of the box. Working on one side at a time, peel the backing off two of the small strips inside the box and the long strip outside the box. Anchor one end of an 18" (46cm) long and 3" (8cm) wide striped ribbon into one of the adhesive strips inside the box.

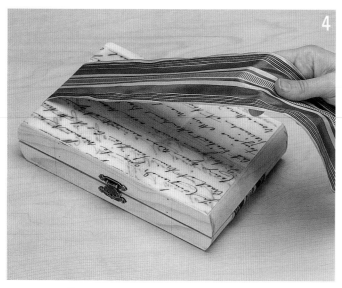

four · Wrap the length of the ribbon around the outside of the box and press the remaining ribbon end into the second strip of adhesive inside the box. Repeat this process to wrap the second length of striped ribbon around the other side of the box. To avoid creasing the ribbon while wrapping it around the box, pull it tight with one hand while smoothing it down over the adhesive with the other hand.

five · Position the frame embellishment over scrapbook stickers so the message is visible inside the image area. Trim away any sticker that may extend beyond the outside edge of the frame. Mount the framed message over one side of the ribbon.

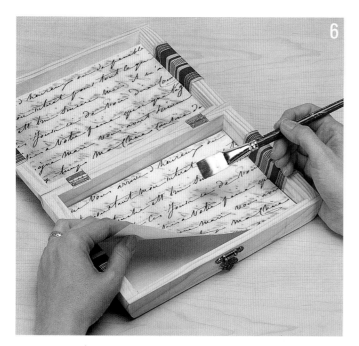

six · Open the box and brush découpage medium over the inside of the box. Mount scrapbook paper sheets over the glue. Brush another coat of medium over the paper to protect the paper and help eliminate any trapped air bubbles. Allow the glue to dry completely before continuing.

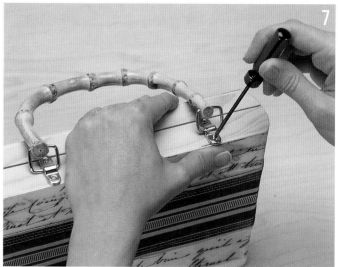

seven · Screw a bamboo handle into the deeper side of the box. It may be easier to drill a hole before securing the handle.

eight · For a decorative accent, wrap a 1½" (4cm) wide striped ribbon around one side of the handle and then tie the ribbon into a bow. Trim the ribbon ends and protect them with clear nail polish to prevent fraying.

ANOTHER SIMPLY BEAUTIFUL IDEA

These purses are just as beautiful inside as they are outside. Select surprising decorative papers to découpage inside the box. The finished purse makes a beautiful gift box that can be displayed as a decorative home accent.

patterns

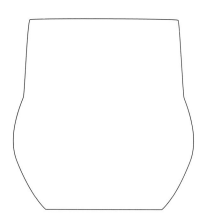

Fashion purse card pattern. Page 62. Shown at actual size.

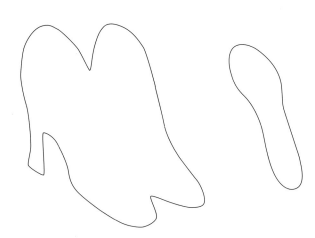

Fashion shoes card pattern. Page 64. Shown at actual size.

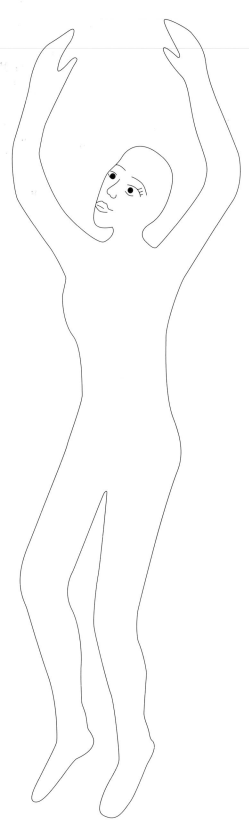

Fall fairy pattern. Page 50. Enlarge 111%

Baby mobile pattern. Page 78. Enlarge to 172%.

Baby mobile pattern. Page 78. Enlarge to 172%.

resources

BEACON ADHESIVES COMPANY, INC.
(914) 699-3400
www.beaconcreates.com
- *CraftFoam glue and Hold the Foam glue*

CREATIVE GIFTED STICKERS
- *Baby photo sleeves and antique jewelry*

DOW CHEMICAL COMPANY
www.dow.com
- *Styrofoam balls*

DUNCAN
(800) 438-6226
www.duncancrafts.com
- *Aleene's 2 in 1 Glue, Aleene's Memory Glue, Aleene's Platinum Bond Glass and Bead Slick Surfaces Adhesive, Tulip Dimensional Paint, sticker sheets and other adhesives and crafting products*

FISKARS
(800) 500-4849
www.fiskars.com
- *ShapeCutter and circle cutter, decorative scissors, hand punches, craft knife and embossing tool*

MRS. GROSSMAN'S PAPER COMPANY
(800) 429-4549
www.mrsgrossmans.com
- *Decorative stickers (pg. 58)*

K & COMPANY
(888) 244-2083
www.kandcompany.com
- *Metal frame (pg. 120)*

LEATHER FACTORY
www.leatherfactory.com
- *Pig suede and laces (pg. 112)*

LION BRAND YARN
www.lionbrand.com
(800) 258-9276
- *Yarn and ribbon*

ME & MY BIG IDEAS
www.meandmybigideas.com
- *Scrapbook paper (pg. 30)*

NICOLE CRAFTS
www.nicolecrafts.com
- *Wooden box and metal handle and latch (pg. 120)*

PEBBLES, INC.
(801) 235-1520
www.pebblesinc.com
- *Color labels and other embellishments (pg. 120)*

PLAID ENTERPRISES, INC.
(800) 842-4197
www.plaidonline.com
- *Decorative and alphabet stamps, ribbon, Mod Podge and Anna Griffin scrapbook papers and stamps (pgs. 76 and 120)*

S.E.I
(800) 333-3279
www.shopsei.com
- *Decorative scrapbook papers and stickers (pg.76)*

WRIGHTS
(877) 597-4448
www.wrights.com
- *Rickrack*

index

THE BEST IN CREATIVE INSTRUCTION AND INSPIRATION IS FROM NORTH LIGHT BOOKS!

· **THESE BOOKS AND OTHER FINE NORTH LIGHT TITLES** are available from your local art & craft retailer, bookstore, online supplier or by calling 1-800-448-0915.

NEW IDEAS IN RIBBONCRAFT

Create gorgeous home decor projects quickly and inexpensively with ribbons! Utilizing traditional, easy-to-follow techniques to create fresh, vibrant designs, Susan Niner Janes provides 25 exciting projects, including lampshades, towels and pillows, wedding keepsakes, baby blankets, purses, desk accessories and much more. A wide variety of styles and helpful templates—even no-sew projects on satin, felt, terry cloth and paper—make this book perfect for beginning and advanced crafters. ISBN 1-58180-351-6, paperback, 128 pages, #32323-K

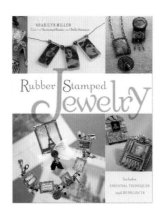

RUBBER STAMPED JEWELRY

Now you can combine the self-expressive qualities of rubber stamping with the elegance of jewelry-making. It's easier than you think! Sharilyn Miller provides all of the tips and techniques you need in 20 exciting wearable art projects. ISBN 1-58180-384-2, paperback, 128 pages, #32415-K

FAIRY CRAFTS

Explore a wondrous world of magic and imagination with Fairy Crafts! Inside you'll find 23 exciting projects that you and your children can make together. Each one features charming, easy-to-follow instructions that are guaranteed to get your little ones thinking creatively including poseable fairies, dress-up costumes, pretty flower invitations and beautiful keepsakes and gifts. You'll also find fun fairy stories to read-together stories that will engage the imagination and encourage your children to create their own enchanted adventures. ISBN 1-58180-430-X, paperback, 96 pages, #32594-K

WILD WITH A GLUE GUN

Designed to inspire friends to gather around a table, break out the projects and create with abandon, *Wild with a Glue Gun* offers a stunning array of craft projects, while showing craft clubs and other small groups how to foster an atmosphere of creative sharing. ISBN 1-58180-472-5, paperback, 144 pages, #32740-K